Bliss Carnochan
9/16/99

Momentary Bliss

An American Memoir

Momentary Bliss

An American Memoir

W. B. Carnochan

Stanford University Libraries

Table of Contents

For Brigitte, Lisa, Sarah,
Peter, Sibyll, and Erika

Acknowledgments

I am deeply grateful to those who have contributed in many different ways to the making of this book, a few of them quite unawares: James and Kathryn Abbe, Sharon Abbey (for her exceptional work as a research assistant and cataloger of family archives), Billy Abrahams, R. G. Abrahams, Jack Bate, John Bender, Norman Bennett, Dick Blodget, Max Byrd, Theresa Brown (who identified "Caroline Testout"), Phyllis Cole, Jill Conway, Cope Cumpston, Gregson Davis, Chris Florkowski (whose talent for organization was indispensable), Peggy Freydberg, Sissy Geballe, Jack Goody, Sepp and Ricky Gumbrecht, Rachel Jacoff, Maggie Kimball, Pier Larson, John and Joan L'Heureux, Sheryl McCurdy, Walter Matherly, Bob Millard, Eugene Olsson, Stephen Orgel, Rob Polhemus, Arnold Rampersad, Richard Roberts, Denise Roth, Dick Scowcroft, Herman and Nina Schneider, Simon Sitta, Cynthia Standley, Hayden White, Marvina White, Toby Wolff, and Gordon Wright.

Thanks also to librarians and archivists at the American Museum of Natural History, the Explorers Club, the Georgia Historical Society, Harvard University, the Huntington Library, the Museum of Comparative Zoology at Harvard, the New York Historical Society, the New York Public Library, the New York Yacht Club, Saint Paul's School, Stanford University, and the Smithsonian Institution.

I'm grateful to Stanford's School of Humanities and Sciences and its Deans who believed that this project deserved support; and, especially, to Mike Keller and the Stanford University Libraries for publishing this book. Andrew Herkovic, who managed the project, was wonderfully helpful; and Chuck Byrne designed the book with integrity and skill.

I especially want to thank everyone in the Stanford Libraries whom I've asked for help over the years. That help has been unfailing and generous. What's more, if not for the valiant efforts of librarians (and others) some of the material (including photographs) that has gone into this memoir would have been lost to the waters that flooded the library in winter 1998. Much of the material I have used is now in the university archives or will be. To Margaret Kimball, the university archivist, I want to say that I know it's in good hands.

Finally, the dedication of this book stands for words that will never manage quite to be spoken.

.

Foreword

Bliss Carnochan's venture in the risky field of academic memoir, *Momentary Bliss,* will undoubtedly delight his many friends and admirers but should attract others as well who have not yet come to know his literary talent and his ironic wit.

All of us in the Stanford community have reason to applaud the appearance of this book. But his memoir will surely have an even wider appeal: explaining how this Professor of English became an almost lifetime fan of the Brooklyn Dodgers and an enthusiastic spectator at a wide variety of competitive sports; how he became a highly successful collector of American Art; how he and his wife traveled to Africa in search of his Uncle (and godfather) Fred, a collector of snakes and snake lore.

Among his administrative assignments at Stanford, he was director of the Stanford Humanities Center for six years. This year he was recalled from retirement as acting director, filling in for the current director, Keith Baker, while the latter was on leave. Bliss has since returned to research in eighteenth-century British literature, the subject that has been his special interest for more than forty years, and, a more recent interest, the history of American higher education.

Momentary Bliss offers us a richly rewarding account of a quite unusual life.

Gordon Wright
Bonsall Professor of History, Emeritus

Dramatis Personae

LEWIS MORRIS *(1726-1798),*
Lord of the Manor of Morrisania,
signer of the Declaration of Independence,
older half-brother of:

GOUVERNEUR MORRIS *(1757-1816),*
patriot and rake

WILLIAM WALTON ("BILLY") MORRIS *(1760-1832),*
who fought in the Revolution, son of Lewis and father of:

WILLIAM WALTON MORRIS *(1802-1865),*
a Union general and father of many
children, including:

ESTELLE MORRIS *(1838-1922), who married*

JOHN MURRAY CARNOCHAN *(1817-1887), a*
bold surgeon of Scottish descent, parents of
several children, including:

GOUVERNEUR MORRIS CARNOCHAN 1 *(1865-1915),*
who raised fox terriers and married an heiress,
MATILDA GOODRIDGE, *(1868-1905) parents of:*

JOHN MURRAY CARNOCHAN *(1889-1891),*
who died in infancy

FREDERIC GROSVENOR CARNOCHAN *(1890-1952),*
"Uncle Fred," an African explorer

GOUVERNEUR MORRIS CARNOCHAN 2 *(1892-1943),*
athlete and stockbroker, killed in World
War II when his plane crashed in
Dutch Guiana, father of:

ELEANOR MORRIS CARNOCHAN *(1916-1992),*
who married a bishop,

GOUVERNEUR MORRIS CARNOCHAN 3 *(1919-1944),*
killed in World War II during the Battle of,
the Bulge, older half-brother of:

WILLIAM BLISS *(1776-1855),*
a poor laborer in Western Massachusetts, said to have
died insane, father of:

GEORGE BLISS *(1816-1896),*
who went to Manhattan and became rich, first
in dry goods and then in banking, father of:

WALTER PHELPS BLISS *(1870-1924),*
self-styled "capitalist"

HENRY PORTER BALDWIN *(1814-1892),*
Governor of Michigan, who married SIBYL LAMBARD
(1841-1922); parents of:

KATHARINE PORTER BALDWIN *(1869-1961),*
who married Walter Phelps Bliss; parents of four
daughters of whom the third–demure and
handsome–was:

SIBYLL BALDWIN BLISS *(1904-1966), who married*
GOUVERNEUR MORRIS CARNOCHAN 2,
(1892-1943) parents of:

WALTER BLISS CARNOCHAN *(1930-),*
author of this book, forty years a teacher
at Stanford, married to
BRIGITTE HOY FIELDS *(1941-),*
a photographer and fellow-seeker
after Uncle Fred.

For the Lambards and Farnhams,
see the final chapter.

Prologue

My cousin and I were born three days apart and each named for our grandfather Walter Bliss. For some reason he became Walter and I became Bliss. I never wanted to be Walter, but being Bliss was an adolescent affliction. When I arrived at boarding school aged thirteen, one of the hearty athletic types who taught there decided I was Iggy, ignorance being bliss. Iggy took some years to vanish altogether. At home I was Pete, as my mother Sibyll had been in her childhood. When I was eighteen and feeling self-important as I signed an occasional check, I became W. Bliss. When I was in my thirties and having to publish or perish, I became, after some hesitation, W. B. because W. Bliss now seemed an affectation, because initials only were the genteel English way (W. B. Yeats, T. S. Eliot, D. H. Lawrence, F. R. Leavis) and because I'd not overcome the embarrassment of being just plain Bliss. Worst of all, Bliss was ambiguous as to gender. Years later when I had come to terms with the name and proclaimed myself Bliss Carnochan on a Stanford letterhead, a letter would arrive once in a while addressed to Ms. Carnochan. When that happened it pleased me by adding a touch of the mysterious to my identity. Finally I have come to like being Bliss, even though I also remain W. B., inspiring the occasional question, what's the "W." for, a question I don't usually answer if I can help it.

The reason for remembering one's past is to remember that you really are Bliss (or whoever) and always have been: in my case that is (or was) a shy, precocious little boy whose school report cards were effusive in their praise, who at the age of nine squeaked into a recording machine that he wanted to grow up and be "an aviator," who grew up and was for twenty years or more scared to death of flying, and who became a professor despite having thought, as an adolescent, that teachers were uniquely underprivileged in having to stay in one place while the flood of students rolled past. Things never turned out quite as I thought they would, but they did not turn out badly at all.

Going to Greenwood

My great-grandfather George Bliss is buried in his family vault at Greenwood Cemetery in Brooklyn, the once fashionable parklike burying-ground modeled on Père Lachaise in Paris and Mount Auburn in Cambridge that in the mid-nineteenth century was "the daily resort of citizens and strangers" (said a contemporary account), "an uncounted throng." With its hundreds of acres, the cemetery still has room for newcomers but is no longer the resort of uncounted throngs. On the wrought-iron fence all around it are signs at frequent intervals that say "WARNING: Protected by Armed Guards and K-9 Patrol." Nor is it any longer reserved for the rich or famous. One March day when I was in Manhattan, I went looking for George Bliss's grave. The driver of the car I hired, Panamanian by birth, was a Brooklynite who knew the city well. When I told him I wanted to go to Greenwood, and why, he said, "Your great-grandfather would be proud of you." It turned out his aunt is buried there, so he had no trouble finding it. We picked up a map at the main office and amongst the maze of stones and memorials in a corner of the cemetery, it was he who finally located the plain, lettered stone marked "Family Vault of George Bliss," littered with dry leaves. He used a fallen branch to sweep off the leaves. "I live near here," he said, "I could get my camcorder." But I decided to settle for my throwaway camera. I took a picture of him sweeping the stone, and then he took a picture of me sitting on it. I doubted George Bliss would have been proud of me but was glad to have found him there, in the cool shade of a large rhododendron at the intersection of Heath Path and Hazel Path, just off Locust Avenue. After all, I owed him the life I had been able to choose: his money, and there was plenty of it, made it possible for me not to worry about having to make more, something I would not have been good at.

On the way to Greenwood, an image of the gilded angel Moroni high on the temple in Salt Lake City swam into my mind. Mormonism puzzles non-Mormons but has struck a vein by joining religion and family history together in a sacred communion. Once I was in Salt Lake visiting my son, Peter, got up early one morning, and went to the Mormon Family History Center. Newcomers waited in a small room until a "missionary" came to give a little talk on the uses of the center and offer the help of other missionaries there, should anyone need it. I spent an hour fiddling with the computer database–so user-friendly that research libraries might learn a thing or two from it–and looking casually for Carnochans and Blisses in the county records and parish registries that filled the shelves. The center was jammed with readers, reminding me of the crowds that filled the British Library reading room where I once spent most of a sabbatical year, all settling in for a day's work or a lifetime's. In this beaver-like activity, I saw a different version of the ancestor worship I had grown up with in the setting of Park Avenue, propriety, wealth, noblesse oblige, family genealogies, and WASP-ish gentility, not to mention the "custom" cigarettes made for my parents and packed in a tin box covered in blue and white paper and with the brand name "Ego." I'd wondered if the Family History Center might yield some new scrap of information that I didn't know, the ancestral past holding out the hope that answers to inarticulate questions can be discovered if you dig deep enough, just as digging in the archives and good luck will sometimes turn up unexpected new knowledge. Arriving from some distant place, amidst the countless comings together, endless copulations, births, and deaths, here you are. No wonder ancestor worship flourishes, even though it may provoke a belated family quarrel. And, after a long journey, you may find yourself back where you began.

It was years before my forbears interested me at all. I had more important people to learn about (Swift, Pope, Johnson) and it was even longer before I could keep my ancestors reasonably straight. On one side are the Carnochans, the first of whom came from the Southwest of Scotland in the early nineteenth century, and who then married, over three generations, into the families of Morris, Goodridge, and Bliss; on the other side are the Farnham family, one of whose daughters, my great-great-grandmother, married a Lambard, whose daughter, my great-grandmother, married a Baldwin, whose daughter, my grandmother, married a Bliss, whose daughter, my mother, married a Carnochan who, between them, begat me.

It is all an Anglo-Celtic mix of Scotland (the Carnochans), Wales (the Morrises), and England (the Blisses and probably the others, too), and, once they had come to this country, a mix of South, Northeast, Middle West, and, where money so often came to rest, Manhattan. The first Carnochan to arrive traded cotton in Savannah and speculated in Florida land early in the nineteenth century after a stopover in the Bahamas;

Allan Lambard made his fortune in Maine; his son-in-law-to-be, Henry Porter Baldwin, my great-grandfather, left Rhode Island for Detroit in 1818, becoming governor of Michigan in 1869 and later a U. S. Senator. But by the end of the nineteenth century, Manhattan had drawn all the Blisses and the Carnochans there. A few of the tribe, like Governor Baldwin, achieved some fame. John Murray Carnochan, son of the merchant who had come to Savannah, was a prominent surgeon. And almost all were rich, some more than others. They were also, in spirit, American Victorians. A biographical notice about Governor Baldwin in 1888 struck the mandatory and sonorous chord: "Mr. Baldwin is a prominent member of the Episcopal church and well known for his many acts of liberality and public spirit."

Only my mother, Sibyll, born in 1904, was a child of this century, and in her bones she was a Victorian, too, though aware that her world was breathing its last in the years after World War II. If that world survives at all, it is in the deep South, where Tennessee Williams turned it into art. At one decaying plantation close to the Mississippi River and to the Louisiana State prison in Angola, the ninety-two-year-old owner shows tourists around her house, pointing proudly to the Sèvres and the Wedgwood and the dirty Sully portrait on the wall, serving her guests cream sherry in tiny glasses out of a crystal decanter on the dining room table. Better, surely, that the Old World should have disappeared as it did in the North rather than lingering on so poignantly. But one of my forbears, at least, managed to escape the Victorian way of life even before it collapsed, though he went a long way to do it. This was Uncle Fred Carnochan, whose world for close to ten years in the 1920s and 1930s was not that of American high society but of African religion and medicine. He was a mid-century renegade, an adventurer at a time when earlier avenues to pioneering, colonizing, and adventuring had been closed. But the Victorian world and the associated scene of high society, with its mixed strengths, foibles, and frailties, was still the setting against which Uncle Fred acted his unlikeness out. It is also the ghostly past I've struggled with in a place, California, and in a profession from which Victorian life and high society both seem distant fictions dreamed up by a storyteller who can't decide whether the plot is that of *Paradise Lost* or *The Way of the World.*

Three Weddings

In Victorian America nothing mattered so much as weddings. If they were followed by divorces or scandalous affairs, it was good news for the journalists, but the Carnochans and the Blisses have had little to offer the society pages other than triumphs of the matrimonial, not tales of faithlessness (at least not publicly) or messy dissolution. By the time my first wife and I were divorced, after my mother died and could no longer register what would have been certain disapproval, it was too late in the day to make much more than a ripple on the surface of the family history–and certainly of no public interest. A divorced English professor in 1978 was as common as chaff in harvests of summer grain.

But I was born when such things still counted. For the first decades of this century, a tabloid that began its run as *The Club-Fellow: The Society Journal of New York and Chicago* and then became *The Club-Fellow & Washington Mirror: The National Journal of Society* was published in New York City. Copies now are hard to find, but the New York Public Library has two or three early ones. One of these proclaims that the journal was sold in London, Munich, Florence, Vienna, Monte Carlo, Paris, Rome, Naples, and (for reasons harder to guess) Bologna. Later issues noted that it was for sale not only on newsstands but on the trains that made their daily runs between New York and Chicago. By 1927, copies cost twenty-five cents. A note in conspicuous boldface at the bottom of the first page announced that the journal had, "as subscribers, the families residing on the 'right' side of the fashionable avenues of New York, Philadelphia, Boston, Baltimore, Washington, Pittsburgh, Detroit and Chicago"–the fashionable world, like major league baseball, then extending only so far from New York as Chicago, a day's train ride away–and that "the field of this publication is at once compact, easily covered and financially potent." The cover illustration showed a woman in evening dress with many a furbelow and a lorgnette casually in hand, a man with top hat and monocle, and a horse-drawn carriage in the background with footman and driver. It looks like *The New Yorker's* signature cover transmuted by the sensibility of a Louella Parsons.

From its start the main feature of the tabloid was a gathering of social notes called "Audacities" that were signed by "The Club-Fellow," a *bon vivant* whose roving eye or roving spies knew what was going on behind many a closed door, who was who, and who was about to marry or divorce whom. The audaciousness of the Club-Fellow's audacities lay not so much in news of births, marriages, divorces, parties, and summer cottages in Southampton as in the high-pitched, gossipy-bitchy tone. In 1905 one Jimmy Stokes was reported to have said of a young Newport woman, known for her risqué habit of crossing her somewhat ample legs in public, that her leg was like the Hudson River: "the farther you went, the better you liked it." Still worse was a long, nasty entry for March 30, 1927:

> Resting at a fashionable hotel on Madison Avenue, an elderly widow, just returned from Europe, is sustaining the shock of seeing her daughter's name misspelled in the condensed list of the society Bible. What difference need that make since the daughter herself once admitted that the Anglo-Teutonic name on her visiting card is not that with which her husband was baptized by pious Polish parents? Although the pair of young people–anyhow, the husband is young–live in a fairly good section of the upper East side, the impression prevails that he has difficulty in supporting his wife in the style to which he never will become accustomed. He is not equipped by breeding and education for his white collar job and might forge ahead faster were he working with the overall brigade. Madame, of course, will not consent to that, but by doing social secretary work she occasionally earns a few dollars. It is rumored that the pair frequently have spirited arguments, the gentleman employing his fists.

The "society Bible" is most likely the *New York Social Register,* with its names and addresses of the upper crust, their clubs and their children and their maiden names (listed under the heading of "married maidens"); for "the Bible" is how it was referred to, with insufficient irony, as I was growing up. Being in the *Social Register* was a badge of belonging, and we belonged. In the 1920s, when one upper-crusty Manhattan banker, later the father of a son who was to become my friend for (so far) 60 years, married the actress Cornelia Otis Skinner, he found himself cast out from its pages, only to be restored to grace when his new wife, having looked at the Bible carefully, declared "there's an actress or a whore on every page" and used her inside knowledge to effect a rapid reinstatement. As for the Club-Fellow's "fairly good" section of the Upper East Side, that might be almost anywhere other than the best locations on Park Avenue or Fifth. But what is surprising, amidst all the fluff in a national journal of society, the Club-Fellow exposes here the dark underside of its world in a vignette that might have come, except for the final, sudden, explicit, and ugly eruption of violence, from James or Wharton: the marriage of older wife and young husband, of New York society and Eastern Europe (could it even be Jewish Eastern Europe, "baptism" or no "baptism"?)–all of it horribly gone to seed and to journalistic outrage, though relieved by a reluctant hint of pathos. The elderly widow, resting on her return from Europe, has more to be shocked about than she likely knows.

Only a little later on in the same listing of "Audacities" in the same issue of *The Club-Fellow* for March 30, 1927, is another item, less conspicuously nasty at first if not perhaps at second glance. As I read it now, I hardly know whether to be angry or amused or perversely pleased. Sibyll Bliss, the Club-Fellow had learned, was engaged to marry:

> Mrs. Walter Phelps Bliss…now surveys life through rose-hued glasses. The rosy halo surrounding Mrs. Bliss's daughter Sibyll is glowing as the heart of a Caroline Testout. Sibyll, the light-footed and light-hearted, has engaged herself to Gouverneur Carnochan, member of the best clubs and one of the town's oldest families, as well as of the Lords of Manors, who meet once annually, without letting the public know anything about that meeting. Sibyll is so many years past the flapper stage that nobody need point out to her the advantage of marrying a widower as well as of getting out of her mother's home and off of the family's charge accounts before her younger sister, Priscilla, must be formally brought out. During four or more years in society, a girl with wide open eyes, ears and mind learns a great deal more than she chatters about… Bliss is a good old New England name. Nobody denies that. The Blisses have always gone about with the better elements of New York. Nevertheless, Sibyll is on the verge of marrying brilliantly– however the match was brought about!

The innuendo is pervasive, skillful, yet not easy to penetrate seventy years later. One mystery (solved by good luck when a friend discovered the answer in a novel by Elizabeth Bowen) was Caroline Testout. She sounds like a racy ingenue from the likes of Evelyn Waugh but in fact "she" is not Caroline Test-out but a popular hybrid tea rose named "Mme. Caroline Testout," satiny pink in color, hence Mrs. Bliss's "rose-hued" glasses and the "rosy" and "glowing" halo surrounding her daughter Sibyll. But even more than Caroline Testout, the Club-Fellow's sibilant innuendo is something of a puzzle.

In his veiled fashion, the Club-Fellow insinuates that Mrs. Bliss must be on the shorts and therefore glad to get one financial burden off her hands, an insinuation not altogether off the mark as I reconstruct the gradual decline of the family fortunes; and, also, that the light-footed, light-hearted Sibyll is not only about to marry brilliantly but, having gone slightly over the hill (she was two days short of twenty-three), has brought off the engagement by good management, good luck, and prudent calculation in landing a more than respectable widower, then thirty-five years old, his standing attested by membership in "The Order of Colonial Lords of Manors in America," an organization whose values can be illustrated by remarks that Montgomery Schuyler, president of the New York branch, made in 1930. The Order's motto was (what else?) "noblesse oblige": "There have been published in recent years a succession of books and articles tending to belittle and hold up to ridicule the achievements of our ancestors and to attempt to show that birth and tradition are of no importance or influence in the world of today." President Schuyler and the Colonial Lords of Manors did not agree: "What is needed more and more in our time is the realization of the ancient sentiment expressed in the motto of this Order 'Noblesse oblige' and its practical application to our lives." Although the Blisses settled in western Massachusetts in the early seventeenth century, they had no manorial lordships to boast of. Socially speaking, Sibyll was getting the better deal in marrying one of the Lords of the Manor.

I found the clipping from *The Club-Fellow* in a small straw reticule patterned with green and red where, with other more conventional announcements of Sibyll's engagement and eventual marriage, it had lain undisturbed for over sixty years. One clipping looked ahead to the couple's upcoming honeymoon: "Mr. and Mrs. Carnochan are sailing tonight at midnight on the *Berengaria* for a honeymoon trip abroad..." Midnight sailings allowed time for going-away parties, though by the time I was old enough to travel (all but once in tourist class) on a few of the great ocean liners, they caught the less glamorous daytime tides. But it's the clipping from *The Club-Fellow* that teases the imagination. Could Sibyll possibly have missed its spectacular vulgarity? As I knew her, she was uncompromisingly dignified, not at all the light-footed, light-hearted, slightly over the hill flapper portrayed by the Club-Fellow, whom she could hardly have recognized as herself. Certainly she was not one to take innuendo gladly. Did she (I recoil from the idea) subscribe to *The Club-Fellow*? Or, if the item arrived from a clipping service, did she bother to read it? Did she read it and decide to rise above its silliness, even despite the parting ugliness of its final exclamation point:"however the match was brought about!"? I wish I had been the reason for the exclamation point and for Sibyll's brilliant catch, but her well-planned marriage to Gouverneur Carnochan, known as Gouv, didn't take place until August, and I wasn't born until three years later.

When Sibyll died in 1966, then almost twenty-five years a widow, there came to me in California, together with the little straw reticule, many a brittle, yellowed clipping celebrating the peacock glitter of earlier weddings in the gilded age. Those of Sibyll's parents in 1897, Walter Phelps Bliss and Katharine Porter Baldwin, and of Gouv's parents in 1888, the Gouverneur Morris Carnochan who was first to bear that patriotic name and Matilda Grosvenor Goodridge, were both grand affairs, and the Bliss-Baldwin marriage was more than grand: it was a civic extravaganza.

Detroit could hardly contain itself when Sibyll's mother, Katharine, known as Katie and the second daughter of Michigan's Governor Baldwin, married Walter Bliss, son of a hugely rich New York banker, at a church which owed its founding to Governor Baldwin's largesse. It was a local triumph:"GREAT WEALTH!" cried a headline in the *Free Press*. "It was Represented at the Bliss-Baldwin Wedding":

> The most exclusive and the most fashionable wedding
> that has taken place in Detroit in a number of years, and
> one in which the combined wealth of the principals was
> greater than any ever celebrated west of New York, with
> one exception, perhaps, took place yesterday at 12 o'clock
> noon at St. John's church.

The toting up of wealth and the claim that the wedding brought together more of it than any, saving one, that had ever taken place west of Manhattan has a certain provincial charm. Then as now, New York was the touchstone, and the great new fortunes that had already been made in California—in gold, in silver, in dry goods—were of no interest at all to old New York or not-quite-so-old Detroit. The groom's best man was his Yale classmate William G. Rockefeller, who was married and ineligible by social custom for the best man's role, but "as he is Mr. Bliss's dearest friend," was nonetheless asked to do the job, thus enhancing the aura of princely riches: William G. Rockefeller was John D.'s nephew. The bride's favors to her bridesmaids were gold brooches "bearing the receiver's monogram" and "studded with diamonds." And many uninvited spectators, who waited outside the church to glimpse the bridal party, "would have literally forced their way inside had not Detective O'Neil, who stood on guard, resisted their advances in his usual good-natured manner." Amidst all the jewels and hats and flowers and splendor, Detective O'Neil, apparently a familiar figure on the Detroit scene, casts an amiable Irish glow like an old Chekhovian retainer. The marriage of Sibyll's mother and father merged middle-western power and wealth to the even greater riches of New York—and assured Detroit that it was a city to be reckoned with.

The marriage of Mattie Goodridge and the first Gouverneur Morris Carnochan who, if they'd lived long enough, would have become Sibyll's in-laws, had taken place in October 1888, at Riverdale-on-Hudson, a posh Manhattan suburb. It lacked the civic overtones of the Bliss-Baldwin union and was more a dynastic than a public event. By marrying Mattie Goodridge, the first Gouv Carnochan joined the lineage (though more modest fortunes) of the Morrises and the Carnochans to old money from the China trade. His bride was a darling of the social pages, which liked nothing more than a pretty heiress. Eight months before the wedding, the *Morning Journal* of New York carried a Sunday feature called "Short, But Very Sweet" spotlighting "Some of the Petite Belles of Fashionable Society," all of them small, though not remarkably so by the norm of their time, all of them rich, and, first on the list, "Charming Miss Goodridge" who comes first not because she is the richest but because she is perhaps "the shortest and the most bewitching"—along with "Bewitching Miss Zerega," "Brave Miss Heckscher," "Lovely Little Miss Livingston," and half a dozen more. Of Mattie Goodridge, the *Morning Journal* reported not only that she was engaged to "the young Gouverneur Carnochan" but that "she has been likened often to a primrose, and she is indeed the personification of some bright flower. She is about 4 feet 10 inches in height and has a graceful figure, slender yet rounded, a sweet face, with rosy cheeks, great, wide, open blue eyes, a little, retroussé nose and"–the *Journal* is bewitched by bewitchery–"a bewitchingly pretty mouth. Then her voice is so low and sweet and her manners so perfect that she is often called the 'Good Princess.'" Best of all:"She is worth at least a million in her own right." Her husband-to-be was a lucky young man and surely knew it.

When the wedding took place in October, the *Morning Journal* announced:"Marriage on a Million" and "Mr. and Mrs. Carnochan Sure of Their Bread and Butter." The groom's best man was one Philip Livingston Livingston, very likely a brother to the lovely little Miss Livingston of the earlier article who had been credited with a fortune of two million, and when the ceremony was over, "the tall bridegroom, who is just twenty-three, blond and handsome, stooped down and kissed his little nineteen-year-old bride." The *Morning Journal* was a few months off: Mattie had turned twenty in March.

Yet there was something about this wedding that, even perhaps in the eyes of those present, seems not quite up to its social importance. Though a private railroad car had brought guests from Manhattan, it was, the newspapers said, a "simple" affair with no ushers or bridesmaids. Of course old money and old families sometimes specialize in simplicity, just as lords and ladies of the eighteenth-century court liked to dress up (or down) as shepherds and shepherdesses. Even so, given the absence of ushers and bridesmaids, the wedding was more than ordinarily simple. And, digging through death notices and birth certificates, I discovered why, though the knowledge (as with many such a discovery) made its presence felt more as a lucky perception than as a hard-earned finding: in short, Mattie the primrose princess was pregnant. Therefore the wedding had to be gotten together in a hurry, even though the engagement had been announced at least eight months earlier. Perhaps the ceremony had been scheduled for later and attendants had been signed on, only then to discover that not everyone could make the earlier date. The simplicity of the wedding was a virtue made out of necessity.

After the ceremony the newlyweds set off to Scotland where the medicine was good and where the Carnochans had come from. Their child, a boy, was born in Edinburgh and named John Murray Carnochan after his grandfather. Amidst the mass of family documents is an "extract entry of birth," in other words a copy, from the Edinburgh registry, giving little John Murray's birth date as May 21, 1889, his father's occupation, perhaps disingenuously, as "bank clerk," and his parents' marriage as having taken place not on October 30 but on August 1, 1888, almost ten months before the baby was born. In Edinburgh the parents could safely say they had wed on August 1, but they couldn't have counted on their prying grandson, a century later, chancing on the evidence with the thrill of having uncovered a family skeleton–not a very big skeleton, to be sure, but enough to satisfy my yearning for something disreputable. Even if my mother and father didn't conceive me until well after the wedding, my Carnochan grandparents, the handsome Gouv and the demure little Mattie, were in their way more modern, if not so modern as to be spared the hugger-mugger simplicity of a prematurely staged wedding. After the not-so-newlyweds returned home, little John Murray died before he reached the age of two.

To the *Morning Journal's* vignette of Gouv stooping down to kiss his tiny bride should be added a more business-like assessment by *Town Topics* on November 1:

> The union of young Carnochan and Miss Goodridge was a very fitting one in point of family as such things go in America, but vastly in favor of the bride as regards wealth. The origin of young Carnochan with all its flavor of the Declaration of Independence, it will hardly be necessary to repeat, as the genealogy of his family, a most honorable one, was well ventilated on occasion of the marriage of his sister two weeks ago. As for Miss Goodridge she is a descendant of the old Grosvenor family of this city and State… She is petite as a wax doll, and young Carnochan is a handsome specimen of the pure American… Mrs. Carnochan will some day come in for a share of the Grosvenor millions, and probably long before her husband is earning a fair income from his law practice. His inheritance from his father's estate was small, as there was a large family who came in for a not over large fortune, as such are rated in New York.

The origin of young Carnochan was "flavored" by the Declaration of

Independence because his great-great grandfather was Lewis Morris, one of the signers, and because he took his baptismal names from the yet more famous Gouverneur Morris, Lewis's younger half-brother, a moving force in the Constitutional Convention, the first to propose that American currency be denominated in dollars and cents, the first American minister to France—a "founding father," no less, and a fiercely aristocratic sort of democrat. Gouv's mother was Estelle Morris, the daughter of a Union general, and his father John Murray Carnochan (of the "small estate"), the prominent surgeon, known to have an appetite for the most difficult, challenging, and original procedures. A marriage of old family to old family, bringing together trade, the professions, the virtues of American independence, and money, was indeed satisfying "as such things go in America," a sign that the god of the New World had ensured things were going the way they should.

A "Secret Poison"?

What lay ahead of Walter and Katharine, Gouv and Mattie, Gouv and Sibyll, were not long lives of ease, though Katharine lived a very long time. Instead theirs was a story of declining fortunes and often early deaths, a story of how high society, that floral hybrid of European aristocratic conventions, American mercantile wealth, and heady reminders of American independence, came and flourished, then faded and disappeared, chased offstage by depression, war, and its own ultimately self-destructive drive. Perhaps *The Club-Fellow* had an intuition, as the *Morning Journal* or any of the papers that trumpeted the virtues of wealth and descent from one of the signers did not, of how fragile it all was, how transient was the gildedness of the gilded age. When I wrote a book about Edward Gibbon in the 1970s, drawn to him by his solitary dedication to a labor of great difficulty, I was struck by his recognition of a "secret poison" lying at the heart of Antonine Rome at the very moment when, he believed, the happiness of the Roman empire was at its peak. A "secret poison" at the heart of the gilded age is something the Club-Fellow could have understood. Perhaps Sibyll herself understood it in some corner of her imagination when she put the

Club-Fellow's tawdry write-up of her brilliant engagement in her straw reticule. Critically sophisticated she wasn't. Her reading came from the circulating library. I doubt she'd ever read Austen. Edith Wharton, maybe, because Wharton and Sibyll's mother, Katharine, both had places in the Berkshires, were probably acquainted, and certainly moved in the same circles; Henry James, surely not. Sibyll had gone to design school for a year, and her school exercises showed some skill. She was very genteel. But behind the gentility lay, however faintly exercised, a quiet intelligence. I am glad she didn't consign the Club-Fellow's ugliness to the wastebasket where it richly deserved to go and where, in similar circumstances, I would probably have tossed it. Or maybe, on reflection, I wouldn't. Much of history is a record of things people decided to keep or never got around to throwing away.

Walter Bliss, whose gallantry and wealth had carried off in Katharine Baldwin one of Detroit's most marriageable maidens, died at the age of fifty-three of a stroke in the New York subway. But he had lived long enough to harvest the benefits of being the son of George Bliss, who lies in the vault at Greenwood and whose story has the "pure" American flavor quite as much as the Carnochan line, though with a difference. George Bliss could have been invented by Horatio Alger, for he was the son of a laborer in Northampton, Massachusetts, who was said to have been insane for the last thirty years of his life, and George had to leave school to work on a farm when he was eight, so straitened were the family circumstances. In 1844, at the age of twenty-eight, "having accumulated some small savings," as the *Dictionary of American Biography* says in Alger-ian fashion, the young man went to New York, founded a dry goods firm, grew rich and then grew richer when he moved up the social scale in 1869 to become junior partner in a banking firm whose principal, Levi Morton, was successively minister to France, vice-president of the United States (1889-93) and governor of New York (1895-97). George Bliss died in 1896, his eightieth year and one year before his son Walter, the child of a second marriage, wed Katharine Baldwin. A newspaper account from western Massachusetts eulogized George as "Northampton's Loyal Son" and celebrated Alger-ian onward-and-upwardness:"It is estimated that Mr. Bliss's total wealth represents $15,000,000–a self-earned monetary success which once more illustrates to the young folks who spend all or more than they earn that industry, economy, patience, pluck, indomitable energy and manly strength of mind and purpose make the steps of the ladder to such success." Alger called one of his innumerable books *Struggling Upward* and another, *Luck and Pluck*. George Bliss, a man of severe benevolence and rectitude who built churches and gave money to his less fortunate nieces and nephews but cautioned a son, then living in England, that in his opinion £400 per year was quite enough to live on, could have served Alger as a model–but of course there were plenty of George Blisses in the nineteenth century, some much richer than he. Compared to the Rockefellers, Morgans, Carnegies, and Vanderbilts, George Bliss was just an average very rich man. And, for all his benevolence, he had the instincts that lead to great fortunes. Once, while working in the Huntington Library, I discovered a stern letter that he wrote to someone who owed him money.

On George's death, his son Walter gave up law school and thereafter engaged only in "managing the estate," eventually listing his occupation in *Who's Who* as that of "capitalist." There was plenty to manage and a life to be led according to canons of official benevolence and public service. The daughter of Sir John Lubbock, one of England's most eminent and public-spirited Victorians–who sponsored the Bank Holidays Act in Parliament that led to a grateful public's christening the first Monday in August "St. Lubbock's Day" and who devised, as principal of the Working Men's College, a list of the "hundred best books" that haunts the academic curriculum still–is said to have said that her father attended an annual meeting every day. Perhaps Walter Bliss's four daughters thought something similar of him, though I never recall hearing Sibyll say a word about him one way or the other. Dead for seven years before I was born, Walter Bliss seemed to have passed far away except as the departed source of my given names. But in life he was a formidable presence, with thin-rimmed glasses and thin hair, austere of demeanor, and looking much older in his official photographic portrait than his actual years.

By the time of his death, his list of responsibilities filled a good-sized page. He was director or trustee of four railroad companies, nine insurance companies (including two in London and one in Edinburgh), two mining companies, two banks, and one gas company. Amongst his philanthropic duties, he was trustee of the Society for the Relief of Ruptured and Crippled (a board on which his father George had also served), trustee and treasurer of St. Luke's Hospital in New York, treasurer of the New York Training School for Deaconesses, vestryman and treasurer of Grace Church in New York, and treasurer of St. Bernard's School in Bernardsville, New Jersey, where in 1904 he created his country estate on several hundred acres of land, with a brick house as ugly as it was enormous but favored by a grand outlook, and other farm and service buildings too numerous to count. He called the estate "Wendover," probably because the Blisses had come from Wendover in Buckinghamshire to western Massachusetts early in the seventeenth century. He was also president of the Riding Club of New York, governor of the Somerset Hills Country Club in Bernardsville and of the Recess Club, whatever that may have been, and a member (merely) of the New England Society of New York. At Wendover he raised Ayrshire cattle and was treasurer of the North Jersey Society for the Promotion of Agriculture and treasurer of the Somerset Hills Agricultural Association. He seems to have been especially adept at being a treasurer, a watchdog, and a custodian of good works.

Finally, like his father before him, Walter Bliss was a director of Greenwood Cemetery. Unlike his father, however, he was not buried at the corner of Heath and Hazel but in Bernardsville, perhaps because Greenwood had fallen out of fashion and because traffic congestion had already made funeral cortèges from Manhattan to Brooklyn a difficult business. At his death in 1923 he was weighed down, again like his father, by mortuarial tributes: "he was so eminently fitted for executive and advisory duties"; "he was endeared to us by his rare gifts and cordial friendship"; and "no cry of distress ever reached him unheeded. His loyalty to his friends was beautiful to witness and to remember." It was not the habit of even post-Victorian obituaries to admit traces of any living, breathing, fallible human being.

Nowhere, for example, is it noted that Walter Bliss found time at least once in his fifty-three years for more frivolous pursuits, belonging for a while to the New York Yacht Club and owning, from 1911 to 1915, the steam yacht *May*, 240 feet in length–a mere eight feet shorter than Jay Gould's "Atalanta," with crew and staff to match. Built in 1891 by G. L. Watson, the Scottish naval architect who designed the "Britannia" for Edward VII, and said to be one of his best designs, the *May* had served as flagship of the New York Yacht Club in the 1890s when she belonged to the Club's commodore Edwin D. Morgan. She was a trophy yacht but a difficult and expensive mistress to keep up. ("I don't know which will eat a man up the quickest," someone once said, "an extravagant wife or a steam yacht, but think of a rich man with both!" Luckily Katie was not spendthrift.) In not quite thirty years, the *May* had six different owners before being wrecked in the West Indies while in naval service in 1919. And, even leaving the expense aside, I think Walter Bliss was not cut out to be a yachtsman. The leather-bound, gaudily ornamented guest book of the *May* survives but has the signatures of only a few family friends and relatives and records only a few short cruises. The yacht was a distraction, and probably the obituaries were right to omit Walter Bliss's yachting life. No wonder, perhaps, he died young. I think the burdens of his wealth were too onerous to bear for long.

Katharine, however, was made of sterner stuff, living on until 1962, forty years after Walter's death, presiding over Wendover in the summers and, in the winters, over two sumptuous floors of a duplex at 740 Park Avenue. A 1995 real estate puff described 740 Park as the "most prestigious pre-war building on Park Avenue," and it's said that assets of at least fifty million were then required to qualify for residence. So there was nothing penurious about Katharine's last forty years, and once when I was young and she was in her seventies, she said to me, imparting to her words the ingenuous sense that "noblesse oblige" was not only grave advice but new, "If you have more than others, then you have to DO more." Hers was still a life of luxury, though much diminished from what it had been in Walter Bliss's lifetime. The farm at Wendover had gone to seed, the *May* was long gone, the house on Eighty-Seventh Street off Fifth Avenue had been replaced by the apartment on Park, and the supply of dollars had dwindled with the Depression. I remember Katharine's unhappiness, in the 1940s, with the costs of keeping up what was left of Wendover and the tax costs of capital gains. At the time I couldn't see why gains weren't simply a good thing. She tried to explain, but as a boy I found it incomprehensible. As the years went by, she grew infirm, and her matriarchal ways more querulous than regal. At the end, she was bedridden and her death a mercy.

By the time she died, I had come to California and didn't go east for the funeral, having a fear of flying that lasted until I took a job in the Stanford administration that required me to travel, a job that I was always desperate to get away from and that I now look back on as having cured me of an inconvenient phobia. If I had it to do again, I would get on the plane, for I felt close to my grandmother, who took me on tours of her lavish flower beds when I was very young. I especially liked the little blue flower called ageratum (learning much later on that its name meant "ageless" or "everlasting"). On her death, Wendover's lands were sold and much of it became a golf course. 740 Park was sold, and some of the furniture went to auction. But there came to me, because I wanted it and because, in the division of spoils between Katharine's four daughters, a process that, being in California, I didn't have to take part in, Sibyll made sure she got it–in her way she was the toughest of the sisters–a long, heavy oak refectory table, weathered and worn, that had stood in the front hall of Wendover. It had been a wedding present in 1897 and had come from an aunt of Walter's along with a card announcing its great rarity, though in fact it is a "made up" piece, with Tudor top and Jacobean base. Its solidity seems an emblem, now, of what made Wendover a secure haven and its factitiousness an emblem of Wendover as itself a "made up" piece, an American dream of England's green and pleasant land. As I've moved from house to house, a dining room long enough to accommodate all ten feet of the table has been one of the desiderata. On one occasion it had to be lifted onto a balcony and come in through a sliding door on the second story, being apparently impossible to maneuver up the stairwell (although, when moving time came again, it went down the stairs easily enough). Someday my children–Lisa, Sarah, Peter (whose real name, because it seemed his destiny, is Gouverneur Morris Carnochan), and Sibyll–will have to figure out what to do with it, which will mean deciding whether any of them want it or have space for it.

If Walter and Katharine Bliss were impeccably genteel, the first Gouverneur Morris Carnochan was a much racier character. Not for him were societies for the ruptured and crippled or training schools for deaconesses. Five years after his marriage to Mattie, twenty-seven years old and already embarked on his career not in law (as *Town Topics* had supposed) but in banking, he was still getting into adolescent scrapes. On January 20, 1893, the *New York Sun* carried a headline "Clubmen in the Lockup" and subheads that said:"They Were Having a Little Lark When the Police Came" and "A Couple of Seventh Regiment Men Gathered In for Snowballing an Inoffensive Citizen-Let Go in Court with a Warning." The story was that Carnochan and a friend named Wainwright, after a party, had been heading home down Fifth Avenue at 2:30 in the morning and had started throwing snowballs at each other when along came the "inoffensive citizen," a "sober and industrious" meat dealer named Stonebridge. In the event, after snowballing and scuffling, Stonebridge ended up with a dislocated shoulder and the young men ended up in jail. Because Stonebridge, dislocated shoulder and all, refused to press charges, Carnochan and his friend were released with a lecture from the judge but not without having given the *Sun* and its readers the pleasure of some gleeful reporting:

> If Mr. Ward McAllister's four hundred could have looked into the dirty, dingy, and malodorous Yorkville Police Court yesterday morning they would have given vent to one prolonged and heartrending shriek of horror and woe, for they would have seen, arraigned before his Honor Justice Moran, just like common tramps and loafers, two young men whom they all would have recognized as persons who have the right to move and do move in the most exclusive New York society. Furthermore, horror upon horror, they would have found that these two young men were there for taking part in a disgraceful street row and for assaulting a meat dealer.

Of this scandalizing pair, the *Sun* points out, Carnochan is husband to "one of the most fashionable young women in New York." That the clipping survived in the family papers suggests that a shriek or two of horror and woe from Ward McAllister's 400 was not a terrible embarrassment—and I acknowledge again the virtue of what is carelessly kept, tucked away for some unpredictable someone someday to see. Of course it is easy to delight in the scrapes of the young and to laugh at their victims, the sober and industrious meat dealers who suffer indignity and dislocated shoulders. Poor Stonebridge.

Carnochan turned to money and banking, I suspect, to keep up with the Goodridges and to escape living on Mattie's money. In all events he was very successful, having (the obituaries said) "a genius for finance" and knowing "immediately…how to handle money to the best advantage." By "concentrating his talents toward the one end," he "accomplished the building up of a vast enterprise," no doubt showing Mattie and the Goodridges that new money, especially in the hands of an old family, was as good as or better than old. Yet money was not his only nor even his most consuming interest. His passions were amateur soldiering in the fashionable Seventh Regiment, breeding champion fox terriers at his farm in New City, New York, and, one has an inkling, women, especially after Mattie died, sadly and suddenly in 1905 at the age of thirty-six. At this point, having made his fortune and neither needing nor wanting more, Carnochan retired, like Cincinnatus or like his own forbear Lewis Morris, to his farm, if not exactly to work the land, at least to raise his terriers, one of whom was a famous champion named Go Bang, "the best wire that ever set foot on American soil," imported from England at the prodigious cost of £500. He became a state assemblyman from Rockland County and in 1908 married Frances Adele Quintard, of whom I know nothing and never once heard a word spoken in the family. Being French, as one assumes, may have been her principal fault. I found her in Carnochan's entry for a Harvard class report in 1911 and then learned, from another class report published after his death, that the marriage had been dissolved. It could not have lasted long, for he died in June 1915, not yet fifty.

From my half-sister, Eleanor, known as Eve, once married to a bishop and generally charmed by evidence of unruliness in the Carnochan line, I heard a story of a woman who appeared after Gouv's death, claiming to have borne his child. If it is true, maybe the woman was quietly bought off, and no mysterious cousin has ever appeared from the shadows. If Walter Bliss died perhaps of a surfeit of wealth and its responsibilities, the first Gouverneur Morris Carnochan died perhaps of just a surfeit–or of loneliness or loss. He was touched by melancholy. In 1898 he wrote in his class report: "I am afraid that, as I saw somewhere, mine is the second kind of an autobiography, namely, an ought-not-to-biography." And in 1901: "I am still on the Stock Exchange, and as far as I know have had no new honors thrust upon me." All of this while he was making millions in the years before Mattie died.

I said that Mattie died suddenly, but maybe it was not really sudden. Dying at thirty-six seems a sudden thing to do, but perhaps some lingering tuberculosis or cancer killed her. The *Times* obituary, brief and perfunctory, mentions no cause. Her two surviving sons, Fred and Gouv, my uncle and my father, were fourteen and twelve when she died –and when their father spent his night in the Yorkville lockup, one of them was two and a half; the other, seven months. Domesticity was not Mattie's husband's thing, and her life as much as his seems touched by sadness, not just in its premature end.

I have a portrait of Mattie, an oval in limpid pastels by the illustrator and society painter J. Wells Champney, formerly professor of art at Smith College, who sometimes signed himself "Champ" and who, in the spring of 1897, had a show of his portraits at Knoedler's, then on lower Fifth Avenue and as prestigious a gallery then as now. The press described the show as offering the world something "it has never had before–types of the American girl," one of them being Mattie. "Artists," the article said, "have given us girls who were always the same and always American, but they were more the ideal of the artist and known as his conception, and the artist, not the country, received the credit for her charms." But "Champ" has done better. He has paint-ed the national character of the American girl:"The American girl, as Mr. Champney is to present her, is a real individual," and the portraits display "real American girls in the different sports, amusements, duties and events which make up their lives."

It comes as a small surprise therefore to discover that among these real American girls, Mattie as well as others is portrayed in fancy dress, wearing the fairy-tale, pink and white stage-shepherdess costume she had worn in February to the most famous social event of the decade–or of the century or perhaps ever in New York's history, the Bradley Mar-tin ball of 1897. In *The Opulent Interiors of the Gilded Age* (1987), which reprints photographs from George William Sheldon's *Artistic Houses* (1883-4), is an unbeatable description of the ball and its excess that ac-companies photographs of the Martin house, notable mostly for its "skillful display of expensive kitsch":

> Mrs. Martin's long-promised attempt to surpass in splendor the celebrated Vanderbilt ball of 1883 was held at the Waldorf Hotel on the night of February 10-11, 1897. For weeks New York's milliners, dressmakers and wig-makers had been be-sieged with requests for authentic costumes of personalities from German, French and British history. From 11:00 P.M. until 6:30 A.M., 600 guests danced and feasted, consuming 61 cases of champagne and $369,000 of the Martins' fortune. Though a dazzling spectacle that became a landmark in the so-cial history of New York, it was also tainted. Led by Dr. Rev. William Rainsford of St. George Episcopal Church, critics condemned the irresponsibility and insensitivity of wealth. Mrs. Martin fired back that during an economic recession it had been "an impetus to trade."

The Martins, richer than or as rich as the Blisses and much richer than the Carnochans, maintained a house in London, leased a hunting lodge in Scotland, and eventually, having despaired of making it any further up the ladder of New York society, moved to Europe for good. Their very American infatuation with Europe took the form of a special passion for the ancien régime. Therefore J. Wells Champney, in representing real American girls, painted some of them in costumes designed for a ball at which, as often as not, participants looked like survivors of pre-revolutionary France and whose formidable hostess had something in common (if not in looks, for Mrs. Bradley Martin was very large) with Marie Antoinette, whose necklace she wore to the ball, as well as in other respects with Adam Smith: the ball was, after all, an impetus to trade. Mattie, on the contrary, was all flowers, fragrance, and innocence, as befitted "the personification of some bright flower," the primrose princess with rosy cheeks who had been so lavishly written up in *The Morning Journal* almost ten years before. *The World* described her costume for the ball, illustrating it with a line drawing, as "a quaint one, with a low square-cut bodice and close-fitting sleeves, trimmed with flowers and finished at the elbows with accordion-plaited frills." The flowers that trim her dress in Champney's portrait are fluffy silk roses, pink with the satiny pinkness of a Mme. Caroline Testout. She also wore roses in her hair, carried a rose bouquet, and radiated a tiny, fragile, wistful beauty such as, it is easy to think with hindsight, was not destined for long life in this world.

Perhaps Mattie's son, the second Gouverneur Morris Carnochan who was my father, strong, athletic, and handsome, was attracted to the ideal of feminine frailty. Like his mother, his first wife died young, only seven years after they had married, leaving behind her Eve, aged six, and a son, the third Gouverneur Morris Carnochan, aged three–my two half-siblings, older than me by eleven and by eight years and tolerantly kind, often in a teasing way, as I was growing up; my sister used to like to lick my nose, knowing she was beyond the reach of any retaliation. And when Gouv married Sibyll five years after his first wife died, his light-footed and light-hearted bride may have already suffered the breast cancer and double radical mastectomy that happened sometime in her twenties. I say "may have" and "sometime" because it was not talked about. Growing up, I knew my mother was different. She seemed to have no breasts–because she didn't–and the skin under her arms hung loosely from her, intensifying her look of tall extravagant thinness, even emaciation. How I found out or realized the truth has left me, as though I shared in the desire to pretend nothing had happened: some subjects were just not suitable for conversation, even if nocturnal scuffles on fifth Avenue were acceptable signatures of upper-class high spirits. Breast cancer and radical mastectomies, on the other hand, like second marriages to wives of doubtful suitability, like sex, like money, were outside the pale. Conversation in the household had an air of manufactured superficiality. God knows what, in fact, we found to talk about, though I remember that Wendell Willkie's candidacy for the presidency in 1940 stirred some political enthusiasm. It was not just the servants from whom the darker realities were concealed; it was ourselves. But somehow I came to understand what was different about my mother and to wonder, passingly, whether it meant there must be something different about me, too.

While talk about money was avoided, sometimes it couldn't be escaped altogether. Otherwise there was no way to explain to me why Gouv and Sibyll and I and my Scottish nanny and my two half-siblings all lived not in our own house but in Wendover during the summer and 740 Park during the winter. In 1939 Gouv wrote up his career matter-of-factly for his twenty-fifth anniversary class report:"Entered business after leaving college. Served as ensign United States Naval Reserve Flying Corp. during World War. Last eighteen years in Wall Street." But the eighteen years in Wall Street had turned into a rough ride, and not one to be described in an anniversary report where one puts up a good front. Early in the 1930s Gouv's firm had gone under, one of its members having absconded with the customers' money. Or so I was told: a squib in the *New York Times* for September 23, 1931, reports that Gouv had brought an allegation of forgery and embezzlement against Claude Birdsall, one of his partners in the firm of Neilson, Burrill. But the amount in question, $32,500, can hardly have sunk the firm all by itself. Worse must have been still to be revealed and kept out of the papers, for the *Times*, so far as I can find, never mentions the matter, or Birdsall, or the firm of Neilson, Burrill again. In any case, the partners had to make good, the Carnochan patrimony vanished overnight, and what had been an ordinary life, as rich lives go, turned into a kind of elegant wreckage.

Gouv and Sibyll then moved in with her mother, who had probably insisted on it, and for the rest of their married life a two-room suite in Wendover and a single bedroom in 740 Park were the only spaces all their own. My half-siblings, Eve and Gouvie, and I lived in other of the bedrooms that both dwellings offered in abundance. What money there was paid my way at the most proper of Manhattan's private schools, where I wore with chagrin, especially when I met bigger, older, tougher, less privileged boys on the street, the little blue cap with the white "B" that stood for Buckley. There was also the Scottish nanny to be paid who had never been let go when I became old enough not to need her. I was embarrassed by luxury and by (comparative) penury all at once: none of my friends lived in such grandeur, though many lived on Park Avenue, but neither did they and their parents live with their grand-mothers, and they certainly didn't have old childhood nurses to be kept out of sight like the madwoman of Thornfield Hall. I was also embar-rassed because my mother didn't seem to have any breasts. It was a matter of not enough and far too much, all at the same time. And Gouv and Sibyll put up with it, I was made to understand, for me; guilt could not have had a better stimulus. Yet there was comparatively little mon-ey, no doubt. When I went to St. Paul's School, I went on scholarship. That was one more thing not to be talked about: to be on scholarship was bad enough, to be a Carnochan on scholarship was even worse.

When the war came, my father reenlisted in the Navy at the age of fifty and was eventually posted to the naval air base at Norfolk, Vir-ginia. I was twelve and spent the summer of 1943 in a tiny apartment that he and Sibyll rented. I watched airplanes flying low overhead and tried to identify them. Once I tried to count the planes I saw in a day and was chastised when I told my father how many I had seen: the ene-my, we were always being warned, had sharp ears. I was taken on a tour of an aircraft carrier. And I watched the station's baseball team, whose roster included the Dodgers' fine shortstop and captain, Pee Wee Reese, remembered as much because he accepted Jackie Robinson's presence on the Dodgers as for his own skills. The team autographed a ball for me that I later gave Peter. The ink is mostly faded now but Reese's name, the biggest of the lot, is still legible. So (barely) are a few others, including at least one forgotten major leaguer, an outfielder named Jim Carlin who played sixteen games for the Philadelphia Phillies in 1941, with twenty-one at bats, three hits including a home run, four strike-outs, and a lifetime batting average of .143. When summer ended, my mother and I boarded the ferry that would take us to the train that would take us back to Park Avenue and, for me, to another year of school. Gouv waved as the ferry pulled out. I looked down into the yellow light and remember him on his way into the shadows. Weeks later he was killed when his plane crashed on takeoff into the jungle near Paramaribo in what was then Dutch Guiana, now Surinam. Sibyll called me into her bedroom one morning to say the plane had crashed but no one knew if there were survivors. I would have rather gone to school as usual and pretended nothing had happened but instead spent two days at home waiting for the news. For weeks after, Sibyll would come into my room at bedtime, kneel down beside my bed, and talk, it seemed endlessly. I hated it, hated her for it, but tried not to let on and to accept her need.

Sibyll lived for almost twenty-five years a widow, never showing interest in any other man, nor I think did any man ever show any interest in her. Perhaps none ever dared, for she wore the badge of widowhood with tenacity and pride, and I knew my hope that she would remarry, motivated mostly by a desire to be spared the obligation of being the man of the household, was not likely to be fulfilled. "Light-hearted" Sibyll certainly wasn't, and I doubt that the Club-Fellow had any idea of who she was, even in 1927 when she was young. But neither was she despondent. Acceptance was her way. She spent much of her days watching out for her increasingly cranky, increasingly ailing mother, Katharine. She was often with her younger sister Priscilla, who had no children but numerous small dogs and whose companionship was tempered by edginess of feeling; she had a short fuse that sometimes burned all the way down. Priscilla's outbursts were never directed at Sibyll, but anyone in the vicinity, including her husband, Bill, was likely to suffer minor burns. Wanting more independence, Sibyll moved out of the Wendover mansion into a small house on the estate where she gave modest dinner parties (cocktails before, no wine with) at which evening dresses and black ties were the rule. After I was old enough, I was often the man of the house at these dinners; the guests, being well brought up and almost painfully genteel, never appeared to find it out of the way. The dinners always ended so early that I thought they must have been social failures. Sibyll served on hospital boards, did handsome needlepoint for which she won prizes, sometimes came to visit me and her grandchildren in California, traveled to England with

Priscilla and Bill, but her life had come to its virtual end in October 1943, when Gouv died and she was thirty-nine. It came to its actual end in 1966 when she died, as if in a long-postponed afterthought, of a lung cancer that metastasized to bone and brain. No doubt it was the "Ego" cigarettes and her own cancerous history that killed her. A sad story, not least because ego was not really her thing.

Home of the Brave:
On Not Going to War

In Marlon Brando's first film, *The Men*, Nurse Robbins chides Brando, the angry paraplegic veteran, for having knocked a medal, perhaps accidentally, perhaps on purpose, off his bedside table: "fine way to treat a Silver Star." As late as 1950, when *The Men* was made, the medals of war, like the names and looks and silhouettes of planes and ships and tanks, were still familiar knowledge, especially among those of us too young to have served but old enough to have studied up on war's instruments and artifacts. Identifying planes during the hot summer in Norfolk gave me the taxonomic thrill that some find in a lifetime list of birds and others in the discovery of some new species of dung beetle. The catalogue of names, as Homer knew and birders know, is the stuff of romance. The British had Spitfires and Hurricanes and Lancasters– and when I saw each of the three flying in formation over the green Somerset landscape in summer 1991, the fiftieth anniversary of the Battle of Britain, I remembered Churchill's tribute to the fliers who fought against big odds. The Germans had Stukas, Heinkels, Messerschmitts. The Americans had P-38 Lightnings, P-51 Mustangs, B-29 Flying Fortresses, and B-52 Liberators, as well as exotic water breeds like the Grumman Goose and the Grumman Widgeon. There were LSM's, LST's, LSV's, PC boats, and PT boats. For a boy who was eight when Germany invaded Poland and fourteen when the war ended, it had been an education in classification and recognition.

Amongst the medals were the Victoria Cross, the Croix de Guerre, the Iron Cross, the Medal of Honor, the Distinguished Service Cross, the

Distinguished Service Medal, and, next step down on the ladder of American gallantry, the Silver Star. The citation awarding a Silver Star to the third Gouverneur Morris Carnochan, my older half-brother, I found in seventeen carbon copies held together by a paper clip that had left its rusty mark on the first copy and on the last. In the harsh December of 1944, Gouvie had been transferred north from Patton's army to a unit fighting Germany's desperate last offensive in the engagement known as the Battle of the Bulge. The citation reads: "For gallantry in action near ✶✶✶✶✶ Luxembourg, on 26 December, 1944":

> During the offensive operations against the enemy near ✶✶✶✶✶ on 26 December 1944, two friendly rifle companies and their supporting heavy machine gun platoons came under hostile small arms, automatic weapons and tank fire, and were held up in their advance. Communications between the force and the Battalion command post were disrupted, and it became imperative to secure the only available radio transmitter which was with a wounded artillery forward observer approximately four hundred yards to the rear. The intervening distance was, to the knowledge of everyone, covered by a number of hostile machine guns. Private Carnochan, a company H ammunition bearer, volunteered to secure the radio. He ran forward into the zone of fire no more than twenty yards on his mission when he was shot down by enemy machine gun bullets. Despite his severe wounds, he courageously continued to struggle stubbornly forward until he was riddled by the enemy fire and died on the field. His outstanding courage under enemy fire, his great loyalty and supreme devotion to duty reflect the highest credit upon Private Carnochan and the armed forces of the United States.

Whose job was it to produce official narratives of such Draconian heroism, its stubborn struggles and courageous continuings? Private Carnochan, a sergeant in his own unit until he was transferred, only survived for twenty yards of a mission that would have had to cover four football fields and back again. How did anyone survive to tell this tale of loyalty, devotion, and foolhardiness? These questions are the nagging undertow of skepticism and pain, but even against that undertow, December 26, 1944, seems the fitting climax to a story, three centuries long or more, of warrior-ancestors in the Morris line that joined with the Carnochans when Estelle Morris married the surgeon John Murray Carnochan in 1856–a genealogy of heroes that I am half glad, half sorry not to have been included in.

Where the warrior strain began is lost to view, but more than one Morris fought in Cromwell's army, and a student of British surnames, no doubt more fanciful than factual, derived the Morris name, common in Wales, "from Mars, Mavors, Mawr, the god of war, and 'rwyce,' war-like, powerful in war," the name supposedly having been given to chieftains known for their valor. A more sober etymology associates Morris and "Moorish," the first Morrises having perhaps been dark and swarthy people. But the romantic association of Morris and Mars, flattering to the tribe, probably was owing to the fact that Morrises were in fact often warriors. In Shakespeare's *Henry V* the stage Irishman Captain Macmorris is a comically pugnacious "valiant gentleman." And my line of real-life Morrises was congenitally valiant. The great-grandson of one of Cromwell's officers, Lewis Morris the signer was commander of the Westchester militia in the Revolution, though too entangled with civic duties to make a military reputation. His eldest son was aide-de-camp during the Revolution to Generals John Sullivan and Nathaniel Greene. His second son became a general. And his third son, Lieutenant William Walton Morris, known as "Billy," was aide-de-camp to General "Mad Anthony" Wayne. All three were cited for gallantry. It's by way of descent from "Billy" Morris that I'm a member, if not a devout one, of the Society of the Cincinnati, the organization formed by Washington's officers at war's end that provoked the immediate opposition of democrats like Judge Aedanus Burke of Charleston, who feared the idea of a hereditary and military-based nobility but whose fears would have been assuaged by the organization's quiet decline, by now almost complete, into ceremonial obscurity.

If not for my brother's death, membership in the Society of the Cincinnati, passed down to me when Uncle Fred died childless, would have been Gouvie's, not mine, and would have passed to his first son if he had had one. In that case the Society would not have had a member who protested the Vietnam War vigorously enough to draw tax audits several years in a row though not to earn a place in the FBI files. When the law eventually enabled citizens to look up their records, I was disappointed to be told I didn't have one. To have been included on even a very long version of Nixon's enemies list would have been the badge of at least a modest courage.

The Morrises thrived in their profession through the Civil War. In the crypt of St. Ann's, Morrisania, erected in 1841 by the son of Gouverneur Morris and Anne Cary Randolph in memory of his mother on the family lands north of Manhattan, are interred at least twenty Morrises, some of them whose remains were moved there when the church was built. I count fourteen with military titles, including Commodore R. Valentine Morris, still another of Lewis the signer's sons and commander of a naval squadron in the Mediterranean in the war of 1812; Commander Francis Morris, who fought for the Confederacy and was executive officer of the ironclad *Tennessee*; Captain John Peter Morris, veteran of the Civil War and "a hero of Port Hudson" (the long, fierce siege along the Mississippi that helped break Confederate resistance, at which no fewer than seventeen other Morrises–according to a computer print-out from the Port Hudson memorial museum–fought for the South); and my great-great-grandfather Brevet Major General William Walton Morris, son of "Billy," veteran of the Seminole, Mexican, and Civil Wars, commander of Fort McHenry at the start of the Civil War, who achieved notoriety while commander of the Fort for denying a writ of *habeas corpus* on grounds that the times were too dangerous and was cited several times for "gallant and meritorious service."

Of William Walton Morris's six children three were sons, all of them officers, one of whom is also buried in St. Ann's–Lieutenant Gouverneur William Morris, one of 150 Marine officers in the Civil War, whose career came to an untimely end when he died, probably of tuberculosis, in December 1865, aged 24. The crypt of St. Ann's is a subterranean barracks of dead heroes. Anything they may have lacked in heroism is decently hidden in that claustrophobic seclusion. The crypt, which has to be opened by the sexton with an ancient key, produces in me the same incipient terror–very un-Morris-like–as I've felt in the sanctuary of a Mithraic cult deep under a church in Rome. Like the devotees of Mithras, the Morrises worshipped strange gods. And for all their bravery, they seem to have been something of an odd lot, too, perhaps a prerequisite to bravery. So the Club-Fellow thought, anyhow, commenting in 1904 that "from the beginning the Morris family have always been peculiar" and reporting, I don't know how reliably, that Anne Cary Randolph Morris "was absolutely rabid on some subjects;

especially was she afraid of being poisoned. She used to have everything tasted before she would allow her son to drink." Anne Cary Randolph Morris, the Virginian descendant of Pocahontas whom Gouverneur Morris married in his mid-fifties, had also, as the Club-Fellow no doubt knew, been thought guilty of the infanticide for which her brother-in-law (and cousin) Richard Randolph had been tried, defended by Patrick Henry and John Marshall, and acquitted, the dead child having been, if speculation was correct, the incestuous offspring of Richard Randolph and the future Mrs. Morris.

The Carnochans who joined ranks with the Morrises when the surgeon John Murray Carnochan married the general's daughter may or may not have been born brave but must have felt that bravery was a family requirement. John Murray Carnochan was altogether a suitable match for Estelle. He had studied medicine in Scotland, New York, and France, he performed a minor operation on Stonewall Jackson who once sought him out before the Civil War, and when the War came, he served as a military surgeon, amputating the leg of a wounded soldier on the battlefield of Spotsylvania in 1864, having scribbled a note to Estelle when he arrived at the front:"massive carnage." All his life he practiced his craft with imaginative bravado, the invention of anesthesia in the 1840s having ushered in a golden age in which surgeons could do previously unthinkable things. He devised massive procedures such as ligation of the femoral artery to cure a case of elephantiasis and complete exsection of the entire lower jaw for post-typhoid necrosis, five times he performed amputations at the hip, and he published a textbook, with hair-raising illustrations, called *Contributions to Operative Surgery*. The *Dictionary of American Biography* attributes the illustrations to his wife, Estelle, "an accomplished artist," on what authority I can't discover; if she did the illustrations, she gets no credit in the text. When Carnochan died in 1887, members of the Medico-Legal Society of New York commemorated his daring. "More than 30 years ago," said one of the Society's eulogists, "Dr. Carnochan was known not only as the boldest, but as the most skillful surgeon in the world." And another told a story:"I well remember a desperate case involving the base of the brain, when I said to him: 'Doctor, are you not going too far?' 'No,' answered he, 'dangers go away when they are encountered boldly.'" Bravado and all, it could have been the motto of the Morris tribe.

What choice did the Carnochans who followed have except to be soldiers if they could? For the first Gouverneur Morris Carnochan, that meant mainly play-soldiering, as he shamefacedly admitted in his class report to Harvard in 1898, twelve years after graduating. He reported to the class secretary: " 'You ask me to write you a letter, but after all what can one find to say. The bulk of your and my spare time is taken up, as you know, with the pursuit of 'military glory.'" Safely imbedded in quotes, Carnochan's military glory consisted in a long string of posts, none of discernible importance, in New York's Seventh Regiment, the traditional playing field for high-society soldiers. The entry reads like the parody of an overstuffed résumé: "Private, Co. K, 7th Regt., Oct. 29, 1890; Corporal, April 26, 1893; Sergeant, May 15, 1895; Assistant Inspector of Rifle Practice, of the Grade of first Lieutenant, 7th Regt., April 28, 1896; Aide-de-Camp, of the grade of Captain, 5th Brigade, Jan. 25, 1901; Inspector of Small Arms Practice and Ordnance Officer, of the grade of Major, April 24, 1901; supernumerary, July 1, 1901; assigned to duty with 1st Brigade, July 1, 1901; Inspector of Small Arms Practice and Ordnance Officer, 1st Brigade, of the grade of Major, Nov. 19, 1901, with original rank. Granted full and honorable discharge April 10, 1905."

Even the academic imperative of research does not induce me to dig up the substance of all this military-curricular trivia. But Carnochan's judgment, that his was an "ought-not-to-biography" though adorned with the making of millions, is a sure sign that money-making and playing soldier did not compensate him for the heroic role he had been denied: rather than being still on the Stock Exchange, he would have loved to have reported some new honors, preferably military, that had been thrust upon him. He enjoyed being called Major Carnochan, and all the obituaries did so, but the title must have struck him with something of an empty ring, given the quotation marks that bracketed his pursuit of military glory, and part-time soldiering in no way interfered with his quotidian life, whether making money or breeding fox terriers. The pictures of him in various military outfits bespeak a self-congratulatory duty-mongering, an orotund selfhood puffed up in costume dress. It is the melancholy self-importance of a would-be soldier whose misfortune was never to go to war.

For better or worse, the next two generations of Carnochans had real wars to go to, but the first one, for my father, was a lark. In April 1918 he became a cadet officer in the Naval Flying Reserve Corps, then in June an instructor in aerial navigation, but he wasn't assigned to flight duty until November and didn't go on his first training flight until after the armistice. The months he spent in Miami from then until March 1919 were pure exhilaration, to judge from the album of snapshots he took:"F" boats and "H" boats and "L" boats and Sopwith scouts, formation flying and Thanksgiving races (seaplanes lined up at a starting line), "the occasional happening" (the aftermath of a crash, smoke billowing from a damaged engine), and, best of the lot, a plane nicely framed in an opening in the clouds, cumulus below, cirrus above, and labeled with gay exuberance in white ink against the black page of the album, "The Joy of Flying." The joy of flying lay also in its danger; and once I heard an old, distinguished flier say nostalgically that he had been flying since flying was dangerous and sex was safe. My father would have been disappointed that I grew up to fear flying, even though flying killed him in 1943. It must have been a sad letdown to give up life in the air and return to civilian routine in 1919 and a position as vice-president and treasurer of the State Pulp and Paper Company.

And, after Pearl Harbor, it must have been with relief as much as a sense of duty that he fought to reenlist at the age of fifty, writing letters to friends already in the Navy to ask for help, dusting off his World War I record, and doing all he could to persuade the authorities he was not too old. Since his fortunes crumbled in the early thirties, he and Sibyll had scarcely had a life of their own. Their bedroom in the winter was across a hallway and separated only by a wall (a thick one, to be sure) from that of Sibyll's mother. Meals in the summer and winter alike were promptly at 1:30 and 7:45, tea at 5:00, martinis at 7:15, butler and maids hovering about. I was still too young to eat formal dinner with the grown-ups and only later took my place in this deadening round. Who wouldn't have welcomed an interruption to so constrained a life, even if it meant living in a little apartment in Norfolk? And if you were a Morris, it was a chance in another generation to act out the unspoken imperatives of the line.

In March 1942, three months after Pearl Harbor, Gouv wrote to the Naval Bureau of Aeronautics inquiring about reenlistment. The answer was "It would appear that you may have qualifications suited to Naval Air Intelligence although you are a little on the old side." What he really wanted was an assignment not to air intelligence but to air combat intelligence, and here the doors were at first closed–though he kept on trying, and persistence paid off eventually. That his assignment, whatever exactly it was, would have led to the jungle of Surinam and never back was the least predictable of accidents.

My brother also had to work to get to war. His poor eyesight would have kept him out of service had he not (as many others did, too) memorized the eye chart and passed the exam. Once enlisted, he found himself waiting in camps in Georgia and Mississippi, impatient for action, sweating in the heat of the deep South. Often he wrote me, in his cramped and squiggly hand, older-brother sort of letters with talk of girls and sports and worldly advice such as "learn to dance well or at least competently (it pays big dividends)," advice that I tried but failed miserably to follow. Once he commiserated with me about some catastrophe that befell my favorite Brooklyn Dodgers: "I feel very badly about the Dodgers–but what can you expect from Dem Bums?" And in a letter from Mississippi, undated but not long before he went overseas in October 1944, he wrote: "I have to spend two weeks training our Army of Occupation fodder"–the war's end was in sight–"and then I'm off to war. I hope to Christmas that this is it and not just another bum deal. I may wind up in the Army of Occupation myself if I don't get overseas soon. Cross your fingers for me and wish me a little luck too!"

This time it wasn't a bum deal, but on December 2, in one of the few letters that he bothered to date, he wrote from France griping about the tedium of war: "This business is really very little like the movies–for every bit of action there are days of dull work, mud and walking–and then hard to find the Jerries–I've only seen about six live ones so far. The whole routine isn't worth the price of admission and frankly I wish that I were home," an admission he could make to me without fear of seeming derelict in his duty. "By the time you get this," he said, "it may be after Christmas. So, Merry Christmas and happy New Year." It wasn't until after Christmas, after he died on December 26, and after I'd been called in by the master at boarding school who'd drawn the unwelcome assignment of delivering me the news, that the letter arrived. Last in the line of Morris soldiers, the third Gouverneur Morris Carnochan is buried in the American military cemetery in Luxembourg, a harvest of plain white crosses, along with others who died in the snow and mud and cold of the Battle of the Bulge, the nearest thing to the horrors of Passchendaele that the second war had to offer, leaving his younger brother to contemplate the strangeness of coming from a family of heroes and of having had the good luck, or the bad, not to have become a warrior.

The greatest embarrassment of my life, in fact, was being (like my grandfather) a play soldier when, aged maybe nine to maybe thirteen, I was made to join a social-military cadre of juveniles called the Knicker-bocker Greys, which performed military-style exercises at the 7th Regiment Armory on Park Avenue and, worse still, paraded down Fifth Avenue once each spring to attend a church service and then paraded back to 67th Street, always (I supposed) to the delirious amusement of look-ers-on. As for the real war, it ended before I was fifteen, and later I was exempt from the draft because the two Gouv Carnochans had been killed: the draft board agreed I was a "sole surviving son." I hadn't been sure I'd be eligible for the category nor even sure I wanted to be. But if it brought on some guilt, it was also an ambiguous source of pride. Like John Updike, I might have had the bad luck to be exempt if I had had psoriasis, not a reason I'd have wanted to announce. Explaining that your father and brother had died was better than having psoriasis, even if the explanation was mixed with diffidence of feeling. While my college classmates went on maneuvers in the swamps of Louisiana or rode out typhoons in the China sea or even fought in Korea, I went to Oxford, itself a somewhat guilt-inducing thing to do because I failed to win a fellowship and had to pay my own way. Most likely I would have been a bad soldier, though maybe, had I then known more about the Morrises, I might have shamed myself into a semblance of the heroic. Shame or fear of shame is a cradle of heroism.

Maybe all this helps explain why I would become an academic off-spring of the eighteenth century. In my junior year at Harvard, I discovered Swift, one of whose rhetorical triumphs is Lemuel Gulliver's meditation on war:"dying groans, limbs flying in the air, smoke, noise, confusion, trampling to death under horses' feet; flight, pursuit, victory; fields strewed with carcases left for food to dogs, and wolves, and birds of prey; plundering, stripping, ravishing, burning and destroying"–often to the entertainment of lookers-on; Gulliver himself has watched "dead bodies drop down in pieces from the clouds, to the great diversion of all the spectators." I also fell under the spell of Samuel Johnson and his knowledge that the wish for glory is one of our vain hopes. Being a child of the eighteenth century means I have taught the classics of mock-heroic, not of the heroic, Swift's "Battle of the Books" and *Gulliver's Travels*, Pope's "Rape of the Lock" and *The Dunciad*, not Homer or Virgil or Spenser or Milton. When I had to settle on an undergraduate major, the choices were classics or English. I chose English rather than classics for two reasons, one of them I now think valid, the other not, but maybe neither of them the whole story. The first, true conclusion: that I could never have taught myself to read rather than laboriously, though pleasurably, to translate Latin or Greek. The second, certainly not true: that nothing new was to be said about the ancients and that doing classics would therefore mean only the tilling of already too-well tilled ground.

But choosing English and the eighteenth century also meant joining those who put heroism into question, and even if I could hardly guess at the reason then, being a freshman who had missed reading *Gulliver* as a child, now it feels like a predestined choice. I had joined the camp of the moderns who knew the heroic age was gone and perhaps had never been more than a necessary fiction, anyway. Of course Swift dedicated his mock-heroic "Battle of the Books," in which Homer and Aristotle rout their modern challengers, to the lost cause of the ancients. Like Swift, it turned out, I had decided to defend the heroic in the only way that was left, finding direction by indirection out and submitting heroism to the test of ridicule, though putting the matter that way then would have been quite beyond me.

The mock-heroic has become our only hope of not losing the heroic. The language of the true heroic, when we try to speak it, turns to the tinny accents of the political, and patriotism, as Johnson said, seems ever more the last refuge of a scoundrel. Even Churchill's rhetoric can seem flatulent, and remembering his grand tribute to those who fought the Battle of Britain, I can't escape second thoughts about the reality behind the rhetoric any more than I can read my brother's citation for bravery without wondering who had to write such stuff. Mock-heroic deconstruction has won. "In Flanders field the poppies grow"–but having left behind the worlds of Greece and Rome, of the Vikings and the great Khan, we no longer manage to make the heroic into good poetry. Bathos always lies around the corner.

Harvard's class of 1914 published a report after its sixth reunion in June 1920, at which "Gov" Carnochan and another classmate carried the class banner in the alumni parade during a driving summer rain. More than thirty of the class had died, some of influenza in the 1918 epidemic, others in the war. An obituary for one who died in combat straddles the thin line between grandeur and bathos. It is the story of a lonely boy who, except for the war, would never have become one of Harvard's local heroes. Anyone looking through the report would have no trouble in finding him, but I would rather keep him anonymous, one more unknown soldier.

He spent his first ten years on a farm by the sea near New Bedford, then a prosperous city, where he learned about farming but where he "also experienced the loneliness and lack of youthful companionship which undoubtedly influenced his whole life." Then his family moved inland nearer to Boston, and he spent vacations sailing, fishing, shooting, camping, and canoeing, being "keen of eye and apt with his hands." But the family encountered financial troubles and "constant invalidism" at home, so he was "brought early face to face with the more serious problems of everyday life. Of an exquisitely diffident and sensitive temperament, his mental view," the obituary says, "was largely affected by the experience of his youth." And he hated, just hated, Harvard:"he entered College with but few acquaintances and no long-standing friends. Sudden contact with care-free, joyous youth, brought at first to his overstrained sensibilities only inarticulate wonder and in some instances even repulsion." What were the outward signs of inarticulate wonder and repulsion? How did he manifest his pain? There is no evidence about that, but the symptoms must have been for all to see. He graduated "with the conviction that he was unfitted to merge with the crowd, and … his college days brought little charm to the following years." But then the war came to release him from his own overstrained sensibilities and, one surmises, from great torment. After seven years in a local field artillery battalion, he joined the Aviation Corps.

In the air he "found his bearings. Apart from the crowd, his high-souled individuality, coupled with a calm, peerless personal courage, brought instant recognition and sympathetic friendships"–and with all that, as if it couldn't have been otherwise, death. The obituary rises to a final narcosis of the heights:"Unfitted for the busy world, an idealist, a dreamer, a lover of poetry and of the great solitudes, his patriotic vision soared ever higher than his plane and, engulfed in the ecstasy of mortal combat, he flew to the winning of the Croix de Guerre, Distinguished Service Cross, Medal of the Aero Club, imperishable fame, honor for Harvard, and to immortality." Engulfed in the ecstasy of mortal combat, imperishable fame, honor to Harvard, immortality. The juxtaposition of ecstasy, imperishable fame, immortality, and honor to Harvard would be laughable if it weren't also heartrending. How this lover of the great solitudes actually came to his death is left to our imagination, as with other unknown soldiers. The strange romance of war and the fever of its rhetoric take place in a realm somewhere over the rainbow, way up high, where a poor farm boy who went to Harvard could shed the bonds of earth and sensibility, finally getting from his comrades in arms the recognition painfully absent in his relationship with his fellow graduates, carefree and joyous, of the class of 1914. What did Gouv Carnochan think of this troubled classmate? Or did they never meet? Whoever may have written the tortured obituary, Harvard struggles to make amends for the damage it inflicted on the New England lad with the keen eye and competent hands.

This unknown soldier's story is at least grounded in reality–he went to war and died–but the intoxication with heroism sometimes topples into hysteria. In the thirty-fifth reunion record of Yale's class of 1892– Walter Bliss's class–I discover an address by another class member, William J. Hutchins, evangelist, author of a *Moral Code for Boys and Girls*, president of Berea College, and, most famously and influentially, father of Robert Maynard Hutchins, who was already, in his twenties, president of the University of Chicago. William Hutchins's address memorializes those of the class who had died, including Walter Bliss, and celebrates the bravery of Yale men: "these men of Yale '92 never whimpered, never asked that death bandage their eyes," and were "fellow fighters for our country and the ideal." In fact the accident of birth almost entirely spared the class of 1892 any experience in the war, which came when they were already in their forties. A few had served and Hutchins eulogizes those who "gave health and life to our country's service." But none that I can discover actually died. Being born at the right time is the best way to escape that fate. But the evangelist William Hutchins casts over his dead classmates a patriotic and military aura, as if all had participated equally in a heroic crusade. Walter Bliss's death, in its mundane setting of the New York subway and its abruptness, makes Hutchins's glamour-mongering seem comical or worse, though not more so than other eruptions of evangelical muscularity. On the train that was taking him to–or from–Wall Street, Walter Bliss had no time to request a bandage over his eyes before being struck down.

As the siren songs of duty have grown fainter, so have the war cries of the cult of heroism except from professional patriots. Yet however illusory these songs and calls to arms and however thoroughly I have yielded to the mock-heroic, I find it hard to dismiss all the Morrises and Carnochans who felt and acted according to a different code and to write off their beliefs as phantasms of an overworked imagination. If heroism seems more than we can aspire to now, I still hope in extravagant moments for a chance to prove myself, if only in ordinary comings and goings, a worthy descendant of so many brave soldiers.

How I Found Uncle Fred—1

When I was sixteen, my mother took me to visit Uncle Fred. She spoke of him in puzzled tones, I thought, maybe with a hint of disapproval, though he was also my godfather. She spoke of his wife, Edna, with what seemed more than just a hint of disapproval. Or perhaps it was only her way of speaking about unfamiliar or exotic creatures. The year was 1947 and Fred was living in New City, where his father had raised his fox terriers, then a small rural suburb of Manhattan though now a suburbanized bedroom community whose residents commute to the city across the Tappan Zee bridge. Fred and a partner had founded Carworth Farms, where they raised mice and other animals for medical research. In June 1945, The *Saturday Evening Post* carried an article about Carworth Farms, with vivid color photos of yellow mice and albino mice and all kinds of mice, that played up the war angle, although the war had ended in Europe and was only two months from ending in the Pacific when the bombs fell on Hiroshima and Nagasaki: "The armed forces," said the *Post* gravely, "badly need mice to test serums for inoculations against typhoid, malaria, tropical diseases, and to check blood plasma." "The laboratory mouse," in short, was "helping to win the war." By the time I visited Fred and his mice, the war had been won.

The worlds of medicine, of science, and of laboratory animals were none that I aspired to. I turned faint when I had blood drawn during the physical exam at the start of every boarding school year, and I experienced the panic of embarrassment when the physician did his mysterious fiddling with my private parts; medicine was not for me. As for science and laboratories, I managed to avoid biology and never had to dissect a frog. Uncle Fred, the mouse impresario, was different not only from me but also from anybody I'd known, and I can believe the *Post's* report that his interest in small animals was kindled at the age of eight when an uncle gave him a pair of guinea pigs. He christened them, the *Post* said, "Sir Joshua Reynolds" and "Sir Thomas Gainsborough" (no matter that Gainsborough was never knighted).

In visiting Fred, my mother no doubt wanted to show her only son that by then unusual thing, another male Carnochan, of whom, I would learn later, only a few have ever left southwest Scotland, where the tribe still flourishes: a web page on cheese-making in Scotland includes an image of "Billy and Nan Carnochan" in the 1940s, busy making cheese in the laborious old-fashioned way. Though I was glad to know firsthand that I wasn't the only male Carnochan in the world, the visit did little to enhance my scientific curiosity but did leave me with a vivid image. Walking down an aisle with drawerlike cages full of little rodents on either side, Fred spotted a mouse that had escaped. Seizing its tail between thumb and forefinger, he whacked its head on a hard surface with a quick, efficient motion, then threw the body into a trash can. Years later, when I came upon Tristram Shandy's Uncle Toby in Sterne's novel, so benevolent that he would (literally) not hurt a fly, I remembered Fred executing the mouse with speed and dexterity that would have done credit to his grandfather, the great surgeon who said that danger goes away when faced boldly.

The elder of the two brothers born to Gouverneur Carnochan and Mattie Goodridge after "little Murray," the bastard manqué, died in infancy, Fred was named for his uncle, Frederic Grosvenor Goodridge, who once went with Peary to the Arctic and who later nominated his nephew for membership in Manhattan's exclusive preserve of (until recently) male adventuring, the Explorers Club–and was perhaps the uncle who gave Fred "Sir Joshua" and "Sir Thomas." Fred went to the right schools, first in Switzerland, then St. Paul's, and then Harvard, where he was an indifferent, mostly inconspicuous student and not a "joiner." His relative anonymity ended, however, when in 1911, at the age of twenty-one and six years after Mattie's death, his father gave him a large sum of money and his wealth became known. The following year he was one of those victimized, the Boston papers reported, in a "rare" book swindle. And in 1913, as a Harvard senior, he created a scandal when he secretly married a woman who not only had been married before but, worse yet, had a son.

On December 6, 1913, the papers carried the news six months after the fact: following the Harvard-Yale boat race in June, always a capstone to the year's social schedule, Fred Carnochan had wed Mrs. Edna Guy Russell, "a divorcée of the Back Bay"; or, as the headline said, "Son of Wealthy New Yorker Secretly Marries a Divorcée"–a far cry from the headlines that had or would announce the Gouv Carnochan–Mattie Goodridge, Walter Bliss–Katharine Baldwin, and Gouv Carnochan–Sibyll Bliss mergers. Fred and Edna had married in Connecticut in a civil ceremony because Massachusetts law forbade remarriage less than six months after a divorce. What helped make the marriage news was that "the young man is said to be enjoying the income of $3,000,000 given him by his father when he attained his majority, two years ago." Three million dollars in those days was big money, especially for a young man of twenty-three: rich and handsome, Fred was quite a catch, though an oddball one. Of the marriage the paper reported him to have said in a sententious moment worthy of *The Importance of Being Earnest*:"I guess father will congratulate me on my marriage. It is the best thing that can happen to a fellow. It steadies him and he will work all the harder to make good, and that I am trying to do.'" Considering that Fred's father's second marriage may by then already have been dissolved, his congratulations needn't be so readily assumed, but hope usually triumphs over experience and very likely he did manage to congratulate his impetuous-or acquiescing?-son. In any case, marriage probably did contribute something to Fred's better performance when he returned to Harvard in the fall of 1913, not having acquired the credits he needed to graduate in June, evidently the result of failures in Botany and Zoology. In 1913-14, he redeemed himself with three A's in Zoology and another in Botany-although a D in a second course in Botany announced a persistent independence or quirkiness, even in the presence of a subject he took seriously.

The marriage in June was not the end of the story. Two days after the first article, the papers again had news of Fred and his bride: probably somebody had known, two days before, that something was brewing. Because Edna's divorce decree, entered in June, was interlocutory and not final for six months, she had risked a charge of bigamy. A second ceremony was performed, once more by State Senator Thomas J. Spellacy, who this time had to get special dispensation from a probate judge; Connecticut had enacted a Gretna Green law requiring a five-day waiting period, and only the special dispensation enabled Fred and Edna to marry a second time, immediately, "beyond peradventure" and beyond the possibility of legal sanctions. They stayed married until Fred died in 1952 but had no children of their own and, for reasons that will appear, spent many years apart. Before he took up his career as a custodian of laboratory mice, Fred Carnochan had another, more exotic life far from Manhattan and its rural outskirts.

In May 1935, the *New York Times* carried a headline "African Explorer Ends Long Study" and, along with it, news that "Frederic G. Carnochan, ethnologist, returned yesterday from Africa with some curious reports on native customs there." "He has spent fifteen years," the article went on, "studying these customs." Now, the headline announces, his African sojourn–which had been in fact neither continuous nor so long as fifteen years, albeit long enough–is over. What the article doesn't mention in its brief listing of "quaint" African customs is that Fred Carnochan, more an adventurer in the Teddy Roosevelt style and more a zoologist than an ethnologist, had during his years in what was then the British colony of Tanganyika joined a secret society of snake men and become an emissary of its leader. A few weeks before his return from this, his last trip, he had published an account of his adventures, with the help of a co-author, called *The Empire of the Snakes*. It had been reviewed in the *Times* on April 28, became the subject of a review-essay headlined "Young Python's Return" in *Time* magazine, and was perhaps what called attention to Carnochan's arrival from Africa, not otherwise an event of much newsworthiness, even at a time when newsworthiness was measured differently from now.

Carnochan's collaborator in the book was Hans Christian Adamson, assistant to the president of the American Museum of Natural History in charge of publicity and later a survivor, with Eddie Rickenbacker, of twenty-three days on a life raft in the Pacific after their plane crashed during the war. That Hans Christian Adamson was a publicity man with a fairy-tale name might make anyone skeptical. And, having myself written a book about *Gulliver's Travels* that dealt with the problem of Gulliver's "truth"-telling, I can't escape unease. Did Adamson, to whom I suspect Fred mostly left the job of writing, let imagination run free? Was Fred's own account, like so many a traveler's story, mostly a fairy tale? I think that mostly it isn't, but *The Empire of the Snakes*, in its boy's-true-adventure-book-style, fits the rhetorical personality of the young man who had said after his scandalous alliance that marriage steadies a fellow and makes him work all the harder. In any case, Fred was back in Africa for the last time while the book was in press. In 1937, a year after his return, he published another book, again with Adamson's co-authorship, this one an oddly fictionalized biographical account of Kalola whose name he elsewhere spelled more accurately as Kalialia, the old man whom he calls the Emperor of the Snakes. To this account he or Adamson gave the title *Out of Africa*. In the same year Isak Dinesen published her book of the same name.

Not that Dinesen was likely to have known Fred or anything about him, or *vice-versa,* and the saying attributed to Scipio Africanus, the Roman general who defeated Hannibal, that out of Africa there always comes something strange and new was probably a commonplace among the white-skinned others who lived there, the sort of thing one European would say to another at day's end as they watched the flaming sunsets over drinks they called sundowners in the patois of the colonial world. Scipio had provided the canned ending to *The Empire of the Snakes*:"As Kalola and his home were wiped from sight by the clouds of dust sent up by the whirling tyres of my truck, the words uttered by Scipio Africanus many centuries ago shot into my thoughts: 'Out of Africa comes always something new.' Oh, Scipio, how right you were!" And the Carnochan-Adamson *Out of Africa* ends the same way: Africa's "moods are ever changing-her tactics are uncertain-and today, as in the olden days, out of Africa comes always something new." Africa's "tactics" include those she uses to fight back against European domination. In this struggle she is "hard, merciless, cruel, and cunning." "But perhaps some day white men will grow weary of imposing their ideas and ideals on Africa." One of the ideas white men have imposed on Africa is Scipio's epigraph.

My copy of *The Empire of the Snakes* is inscribed with a firm hand "To my Godson" and signed not just Uncle Fred but "Uncle Fred," as if he were playing one unfamiliar kinship role and I, his godson and nephew, another. Perhaps the taxonomic habits of the naturalist are at work, and Fred was certainly not prone to any excess of familial affection. I don't recall when he gave me the book, but chances are it was on the visit to his laboratory when he bashed the vagrant mouse: I seldom saw him otherwise. On the same visit he gave me a gold-plated medallion that his father had received for academic performance in school, a fact I'm sure of only because a note in my mother's handwriting identifies the date of the gift. More self-conscious as a writer than Fred, I wonder whether he would have cared that his bashing the mouse stuck in my memory as the gift of his book did not.

One can't help approaching the book warily, and not just because of doubts about its veracity. The accents are so genteel ("Oh, Scipio, how right you were"), and the attitudes of someone born late in the nine-teenth-century to Africa and its peoples, no matter how benign, are bound to be discomforting. The complacent, elitist, nationalistic, self-congratulatory outlook of European colonialism, which set off the late nineteenth-century unseemly "scramble" for Africa, by no means gave way after the first war. Colonialism was still vigorous in the 1920s, un-aware of its fragility and failings, still lording it over lesser breeds and lesser lands. It would take another war to change things. The native ser-vants and bearers, of whom Fred had many, are inevitably "boys." Yet it's also true that Fred Carnochan, as much as anyone could short of taking up permanent life in Africa, felt a kinship with the Wanyamwesi people, even to the point of finding in Kalialia a substitute father for the one he had hoped to please, or at least not too greatly displease, when he wed Edna in 1913, and who had died when Fred was a year out of college. Not only does *Out of Africa* end with the hope that whites will stop imposing their will on Africa but in 1938 Fred reviewed a his-tory of East Africa for the journal of the Explorers Club, criticizing it as written "entirely from the white viewpoint."

But from the ethnographic and from the human angle, the question of the narrative's truthfulness counts most. There is no telling, especially since he was away while the book was in press, how much attention Fred paid to details, how much he embroidered reality in telling his sto-ry to Adamson, or how much Adamson embroidered on what Fred told him. Anthropologists have unanimously doubted that the snake guild was a pan-tribal or, as Fred comes near to claiming, a pan-African orga-nization:"I dare say that, if one knew where to look, he would find snake lodges from Cairo to Capetown." But snake lodges, according to the anthropologists, have no affiliations other than the local and are not secret, and one distinguished anthropologist has questioned the truthfulness of the whole narrative, while in 1949 a curator at the American Museum of Natural History said guardedly to an inquiring correspondent that The *Empire of the Snakes* contained "many statements that remain to be substantiated."

The scholar's rule is: be cautious and above all avoid being fooled, so many are the fakes and hoaxes that litter the historical path. Nobody wants to be taken in by the next Ossian or the next Piltdown man or the next Tasaday tribe (if the Tasaday were in fact a hoax). It is safer to err on the side of skepticism than credulity. Yet there's no doubt that Fred spent years in Africa, the artifacts he gave to Harvard's Museum of Comparative Zoology are (surely) the real thing, and so (surely) are photographs of Wanyamwesi shrines and ceremonies (published in *Out of Africa*) now in the archives of the Explorers Club. Whatever may be accurate or inaccurate, hyperbole or sober fact, in Fred's account of his adventures, it is not a Gulliverian hoax. And when I asked a member of the Wanyamwesi, born in Tanzania but then living in California, whether Fred's story sounded "right," he said it did and that even if the lodges are only local now, Africa is no longer what it was. He also said of Fred Carnochan: "He was a very brave man."

"He was a very brave man" and so, another of the Morris tribe. In the first war he joined up as a private in 1917 and then transferred to the Signal Corps as a photographer, spending the war as a photographic nomad traveling between different units of the American Expeditionary Force. His bravery was that of solitary adventuring rather than fighting wars and he more than intrigued me. I wondered if I might somehow find this elusive person who had puzzled me even when I was sixteen. I fancied myself Stanley searching for Livingstone–notwithstanding the staginess of Stanley's journalistic extravaganza. But that meant reading again, after many years, *The Empire of the Snakes*.

"For weeks on end I had explored northwestern Tanganyika for snakes and with disheartening results. True, I had gathered a few dozen mambas, cobras, puff-adders and pythons. Enough, perhaps to satisfy the ordinary collector, but far from the goal set by the Smithsonian-Chrysler Expedition..." With this self-romanticizing of the hero, all of it a mixture of Ernest Hemingway, whose bulls and bullfighters are a rough equivalent of Fred's snakes and snake-men, and a latter-day Horatio Alger hero, whose luck and pluck have nothing to do with money-making, Carnochan's story begins. He is no ordinary collector satisfied with a few dozen mambas, cobras, puff adders, and pythons but one with a huge appetite, a Hercules of herpetologists. *The Empire of the Snakes* tells the story of how he got all the snakes he wanted-and became an overlord of mambas, cobras, puff adders, and pythons by initiation into the mysteries of their society.

It was 1926 (a year that comes beautifully alive in my colleague Sepp Gumbrecht's chronicle *In 1926*) when Fred first went to Tanganyika with the Smithsonian-Chrysler expedition that eventually brought back 1700 live animals, including giraffes, impalas, a kudu, and an eland, among other large mammals, plus quantities of smaller mammals, birds, and reptiles. Fred had taken a Master's degree at Harvard, publishing a few papers on what he called a "little known family of beetles," and his fellow students had included William Mann, a Stanford graduate who by 1926 was director of the Washington Zoo and leader of the expedition. Fred volunteered to pay his own way, no doubt because he could afford it and perhaps because the expedition was short on funds until the Chrysler Corporation agreed to sponsor it (those being days when collecting animals for zoos carried no burden of ecological incorrectness and cost far less than now: for $50,000 Chrysler got its name attached to the expedition). And Mann took Fred up on the offer: "Dear Freddy," he wrote, "I take it you were serious when you said you would like to accompany the Expedition to East Africa."

But why, when Fred reached his destination in the countryside near Tabora in the middle of Tanganyika, could he find no snakes? Getting no cooperation "from my own boys and other natives," he decides they are afraid though not, he learns, of snakes. Rather, of "the Snake-Men, members of the Secret Empire of the Snakes"–it is this upper-case version of the "Secret Empire" that has put off the anthropologists– "who had an absolute monopoly on the catching and killing of serpents." The snake-men are tough operators, zealous guardians of their privilege, unwilling to brook competition. Fred's task therefore becomes to find snakes by finding the snake-men.

Adopting the peremptory manner of a colonial-in-charge, a role he was probably good at, he tells the paramount chief of the Wanyamwesi what he is looking for. The chief claims to know nothing of snake-men, but when Fred says he will tell the British commissioner if he doesn't get what he needs (telling the commissioner is the last thing he wants to do, and the British throughout are basically the bad guys because they have forced the Empire underground), the chief becomes more helpful: because Fred speaks Nyamwesi "as would a friend" and because he treats the chief's subjects well, "'I will send out word and we will see.'" So Fred waits, and in a few weeks there arrive Sefu and Nyoka ("the snake"), bringing with them two large boxes, filled with "dozens of snakes of several kinds, all colours and many sizes, balled up like odds and ends of vari-coloured silk." These are snakes as Fred the heroic herpetologist wants them: by the yard.

How much do the snake-men expect for their cargo? Nyoka, Sefu, and Fred settle on a penny a foot, but then how to calculate the combined length of night adders, boomslanges, cobras, and the rest, "all deadly, all angry and all valuable," and all adding to the epic nature of the quest? To Fred's wonderment, Sefu and Nyoka grab the snakes by the neck with their bare hands, yank them out, and stretch them on the ground to be measured "like salesgirls measure ribbons" as Fred keeps track of the yardage. Every so often a snake drives its fangs, to no effect, into the arm of Nyoka or Sefu, identified now as Nyoka's assistant: they are invulnerable, protected as if by some hidden talisman. In the end Fred pays 157 pence for 157 feet of snakes and offers Nyoka and Sefu employment at 15 shillings a month. They accept, and over the next few years and at least two more trips to Tanganyika, the story unfolds.

Once when Fred, Nyoka, and Sefu are hunting snakes, a mamba, notably dangerous, streaks into a hole, Nyoka reaches in after it, and grabs it by the tail, intending in his usual mamba-catching manner to swing it around his head and (like Fred and the vagrant mouse) stun it on the ground. But the mamba, whirling itself "into a corkscrew," drives his fangs into Nyoka's leg. Fred grabs a knife to slash the wound and try to suck the venom out. Taking the mamba by the neck and pulling the fangs out of his leg, Nyoka laughs and, in the Carnochan-Adamson account, makes a speech in the style of Hollywood-colonial: "'Forgive me, B'wana…I meant no offence, but it was so funny! You see, B'wana, no snake, not even the koboko (meaning mamba), can hurt me… But with the sting of the serpent, came the proof of B'wana's friendship and I will always remember that B'wana wanted to save my life.'" Whatever Nyoka actually said, Carnochan's knowledge of the language of the Wanyamwesi seems to have served him well again: "'You speak the language of our tribe. You are a just master and a good friend. In your own country, you should be a good chief, for a good chief will risk his life for his men, such as you were willing to do for me this afternoon.'" It could be a story of how Fred's great-grandfather, the Indian-fighting General Morris, went to Africa and instead of fighting the natives became their friend. Nyoka promises to ask Kalialia, "the Old One," for permission to tell Carnochan the medical secrets of the Snakes, and in time this leads to Kalialia himself; Nyoka, it turns out, is the oldest son of Kalialia's oldest sister, hence his hereditary successor.

Almost two years pass after the Smithsonian-Chrysler expedition takes its trophies home before Fred returns to Africa in summer 1928, having cabled the British commissioner in Tabora to ask that Nyoka expect him in two months. When the ship docks in Dar es Salaam, Nyoka is there waiting, having walked the thousand or so kilometers from Tabora. That Nyoka walked so far is credible: walking long distances is common in Africa. But Fred, or Adamson, much exaggerates the distance, calling it "nearly a thousand miles," a strange error in an account that claims scientific accuracy, even if we suppose that one of its authors momentarily mixed up kilometers and miles. Nor is it the only error of its kind.

Nyoka lives in the village of Mawere Shamba ("Millet Farm"), south of Tabora, where the villagers have built Fred a house, a grass hut "about eighteen feet long and ten feet wide"; in the usual way of travelers' tales, measurement gives authenticity. Yet I have to get ahead of myself here so as not to suppress more evidence of uncertain reliability in the narrative. From Tabora to Mawere Shamba, Fred reports, is eighty miles and six hours by road, a journey that he makes with fourteen "boys" and a year's worth of supplies "for I had made up my mind that I would bury myself in the heart of native Africa and devote myself exclusively to the pursuit of the history and medicines of the Snakes." But I was to learn that Mawere Shamba or, as will appear, the place where Mawere Shamba was, is no more than forty or fifty kilometers and about an hour's car ride from Tabora on roads that are probably not much better than in the 1920s. I want to attribute the lapse to Adamson, even though he and Fred would both have had an interest in establishing the remoteness of Mawere Shamba. Still I don't think the lapse compels us to doubt everything. Fred had too little guile to be Gulliver. And in a little while ("bado kidogo") the old man Kalialia comes to Mawere Shamba, strikes up a friendship with Fred, and one day asks, "Would you like to become a member of the Snake-People?"

Brave or no, Fred is wary but decides to go through with it, encouraged by Kalialia's readiness to accept some compromises and shortcuts, most likely a result of the old man's desire to enhance his prestige and shore up his power, dwindling as a result of his age and of the British sanctions, by enlisting an eager "European" student on his side. Instead of having tiny incisions made all over his body, then smeared with the preparation that gives the snake-men immunity to venom, Fred is allowed to settle for a few slashes on the forearm. Instead of keeping the preparation on for three days, as Kalialia instructs him, he washes it off as soon as he can. And instead of having to undergo the initiation ceremony, he is offered an initiation (said to be that of a chief) by proxy. Standing proxy for Fred, however, means sharing a white man's soul, and finding someone willing to risk the displeasure of ancestral spirits is not easy. But eventually a volunteer turns up, "a gaunt, hollow-chested man" named Mali Fesa, whose family fortunes have waned after completing his studies in the medicine of the Snakes and, in the nine years since, has been unable to afford the initiation fee of ten bullocks. Fred agrees to pay for Mali Fesa, but instead of ten bullocks, Kalialia settles for a ceremonial two shillings: the old man must have been very eager to get Fred aboard. Then the initiation proceeds, Mali Fesa undergoing its ordeals in Fred's place.

The first ordeal is to spend a night with a belt of thorns, six inches long, braided tight about the initiate's waist:"There are no thorns like African thorns and each of those that encircled poor Mali Fesa was an inch long"–probably from the "whistling" acacia that grows everywhere on the African uplands–"strong as steel and sharp as a surgeon's needle." "Looking closer," Fred says, "I noticed countless punctures and rivulets of blood where the barbs had pressed through the skin." Later in the ceremonies the initiate, his back smeared with medicinal ointment, lies on a bed of the same thorns, this time without pain: the medicine of the Snakes is powerful. The second, potentially lethal ordeal is to capture a cobra bare-handed, and Fred wonders what will happen if things turn out badly:"'Supposing Mali Fesa dies? What then? How would that affect me?'" The answer is disquieting: "'B'wana's soul will have gone with Mali Fesa's, for in the Snakes you are twins and twins have only one soul between them.'" "'If Mali Fesa should die,'" Kalialia warns, "'I would urge that you leave Mawere Shamba at once and go from Africa as quickly as you can.'" Not to leave would be courting retribution from those who believe "'that Mali Fesa died because you, a white man, were told the secrets of the Snakes.'" Who these potential enemies may be, we don't find out. All goes well, the cobra submits to Mali Fesa, Fred assumes his new guild name of Ndilema, "Young Python," and becomes not only Kialalia's emissary to other Snake lodges, charged with seeing that their ceremonies are being properly carried out, but a local celebrity as well.

Once when he is in Mwanza, a bustling commercial port on the southern shore of Lake Victoria, so many Africans crowd into the city to see him that the British provincial commissioner, who speaks a parody version of British-colonial-talking-to-fellow-white-man—"Listen, old chap, we are good friends, and you would do me a great favor by moving out of town"—offers him a vacant cantonment of the King's African Rifles on the outskirts to set up camp. Fred agrees, only to find he is being followed about:"By night, at least three thousand natives were encamped in the vicinity, and on the following day, fully as many more moved in." "Each of the three principal secret orders was represented—the Snakes, the Porcupines and the Women's Guild," and there follow three days of drumming, dancing, and singing, "fires flaring and crackling all night," a scene that could have come from Dinesen. Fred calls it a "round-the-clock nightmare" but surely protests too much. Even if there aren't 6,000 of the Wanyamwesi on hand, as is likely given the difficulty of getting crowd sizes right, not to mention the exaggerations elsewhere, there must have been a great many who had come to see this white medicine man, and I suspect Fred was not impervious to the enticements of fame. He had something to prove, if only to himself, this young man whose marriage had "steadied" him and inspired him to "work all the harder to make good." There in the center of Africa, surrounded by the thousands who had come to see him, Fred must have felt he had made good in his own way, the imperatives of being a warrior having taken in him unpredictable forms of expression.

And he *was* brave. Not only did joining the Snakes entail risk, he also came close to losing his life in a porcupine-hunting exploit prompted by the urgings of a member of the porcupine society ("whose name I have forgotten"), an exploit to terrify any claustrophobe. African porcupines are much larger than their North American cousins and have formidable, spikily beautiful quills. The way to hunt them is to slither down a hole in the earth, spear in hand, and skewer the porcupine at the end of its lair, provided you don't meet an intruding python in the way. Fred decided to try it, first sending a boy down the hole to investigate and clear the path. When the boy returned and reported a porcupine at the end of the lair, it was Fred's turn: "I almost stood on my head for the first twelve feet, then the tunnel suddenly straightened out at right angles and as I am of short and stocky build, it was quite a backbreaking job to get through. I squirmed. Wiggled. Dug with my fingers and pushed with my feet. At last I got into a straight corridor which was lit for a few feet by the light that came down through the hole. I crawled on. I was in utter darkness." And then the earth collapses behind him: "I fought fiercely a head-long impulse to push my way out backward, for I knew that it might bring about another avalanche of dirt." Instead he presses on, hoping there will be space to turn around in at the end of the tunnel. He spears the porcupine, killing it, but finds no turning room. He crawls out backward, pulling the porcupine along with him. He hears voices. "One of the boys was clearing the tunnel. Now I felt a rush of air." But he has to wait fifteen minutes before being fully dug out of the dirt, "handful by handful," bitten by swarms of ticks but bringing with him a forty-pound prize.

The Empire of the Snakes begins with Fred telling Adamson over drinks one evening in Manhattan: "I have a feeling that Kalola is dead," and on his last trip to Africa, he learns that Kalialia had in fact died in the spring of 1933. In autumn 1934, he visited Kalialia's grave and took part in a memorial ceremony. Then in the spring he returned home for the last time, soon afterwards settling into his life as custodian of the mouse farm. When he died in August 1952, his will (which I located with help from a private detective who advertised in the Rockland County yellow pages) left his "beloved wife" Edna all his property, including land in New City, $19,000 in securities, $13,000 in life insurance, $7,000 in cash, and a 1947 Plymouth valued at $600. Of the $3,000,000 that his father was said to have given him when he turned twenty-one, there was no trace. Not even the proceeds of the mouse farm, which he had sold before his death, seem to have survived him. What he did with it all, assuming the story of his grand patrimony was true, I can't imagine. He would have been hard put to spend $3,000,000 on his African adventures. But whatever happened to the money, Fred lived the way he wanted to. During his African years he took a long circular journey, he says of 20,000 miles but I suspect exaggeration again, through Kenya, southern Ethiopia, the southern Sudan, Ruanda, and the eastern Congo. He had noticed that the language used in the ceremonies of the Snakes was different from the usual tribal language and in his journey hoped to learn more about African tongues. Reading *The Empire of the Snakes*, I decided I would go to Africa some day and see if I could find any traces of Fred on his cherished ground.

The Little Victims Play

When Mattie's husband appeared in Yorkville Police Court after his undignified night in the lockup, the newspaper noted his athletic skill sardonically. The meat dealer Stonebridge, angry at the snowballing of his family and his horse, had taken his whip to Carnochan and his fellow prankster, "distributing lashes right and left on their faces, about their shoulders and legs... Mr. Carnochan, who got several goodly blows, made a dash for the meat dealer. Now, Mr. Carnochan's ability at wrestling was the talk of the college when he was at Harvard, and he has kept in training. Down went the meat dealer in beautiful style, with Mr. Carnochan, much disarranged as to his clothing, on top of him. Mr. Carnochan had finished the meat dealer in one round, for Stonebridge lay helpless on the sidewalk with a dislocated shoulder." Carnochan's wrestling skills are attested by a silver-plated goblet that stands on my desk, his prize from the Harvard Athletic Association for a first in featherweight wrestling at the "winter meeting" of March 11, 1882. That he wrestled as a featherweight doesn't surprise me, and the newspaper report of his marriage that said he was "tall" as well as blond and handsome probably didn't have it quite straight. No doubt he was taller than little Mattie, but neither of their sons was tall and Gouv Jr. was not as tall as his bride, Sibyll. My sister, Eve, was very short. Of all the Carnochans, I seem to have turned out the only tall one, an inheritance from the maternal side. But I'd have preferred it if, instead of being tall and what I'm sometimes told is handsome (though I have trouble seeing it in the mirror), the pool of genes that flowed down to me had produced athletic skill–which it didn't do, not in any degree adequate to my longings. Unlike the inwardness of intellectual performance, rare athletic talent throws off a radiant beauty. In another life I would like to be Michael Jordan with the knowing smile and the incomparable talent.

All three Gouverneur Morris Carnochans were athletes: my grandfather, the wrestler; my father, who played soccer, hockey, and after college, polo; my brother, who played some college soccer. My father was the best of them and hoped I would follow him, as I desperately wanted to. When I was eight or nine, he cut down a polo mallet and had me hitting balls on the Wendover lawn, a variation on the American trope of fathers playing catch with their sons. But polo was a middle-aged avocation for him, and it was hockey he excelled at, beginning at the school *Time* once called haughty, hockey-playing St. Paul's. He was a goalie, most vulnerable of positions, especially before goalies began wearing heavy padding and fiercely colorful plastic masks, the modern equivalents of medieval armor. One newspaper account described an uncomfortable moment that wouldn't have happened if the goalie's equipment then had been what it is now: "Carnochan…was doubled up for five minutes as the result of stopping the puck as it sailed through the air, headed straight for the cage. The hard rubber hit the goal tender squarely in the middle of the stomach, and Carnochan's gulps as he struggled for breath could be heard all over the rink." Was it really the stomach the puck hit squarely in the middle of? Or a more vulnerable part? In his senior year at Harvard, Gouv played a famous game against Princeton, led by Hobey Baker–Hobart Amory Hare Baker–his former teammate at school and future teammate for St. Nicholas in the Amateur Hockey League, to this day said to be the best American-born hockey player ever, described over and over as "indomitable," "peerless," "redoubtable," "marvellous," and, in a St. Paul's obituary when he crashed while flying after war's end in France, "brave, simple, human, true–a perfect Christian gentleman," as perhaps he truly was. The Boston papers called the Harvard-Princeton game "the most exciting and nerve racking…that has ever been witnessed on the local rink." Harvard beat Baker and Princeton 2-1 after twenty-three minutes and forty seconds of overtime, and Carnochan starred: "Harvard can thank Carnochan, its snappy blonde goal tender, as much as anybody for the victory scored over the Tigers. His work at the net was something out of the ordinary… In the sudden death session he made four of the most remarkable stops"–two of them against Baker–"that the fans have seen in many a day." When it was over "the players could hardly stand on their skates," and the 6,500 spectators "were exhausted because of the intense and high pitch of excitement which reigned throughout the entire evening."

Carnochan was named best college goalie in 1914 and best goalie in the Amateur Hockey League when he played later for St. Nicholas in Manhattan. The league was made up of six teams (including the Boston Athletic Association and the Irish-American Athletic Club), of which St. Nicholas was by far the most upper-crusty, as a 1916 piece in *The Brooklyn Eagle* reported tongue-in-cheek: "There is a saying in the St. Nicholas Hockey Club that the team never wins the championship unless three members regularly report for practice dressed either in dinner clothes or more formal togs." And their goalie, the first in the Amateur League "to throw the light of a higher education upon the position," was a prime exhibit: "If you ever read the society page, no doubt you have often seen the name. Possibly you never before connected Gouverneur Morris Carnochan with Carnochan the St. Nicholas hockey player. Still they are one and the same and either on the ice of a hockey rink or the floor of a ballroom, Carnochan is one of the best of good fellows"–as well as being "just the very best little goalkeeper in the Amateur Hockey League." The goalie's stick he used against Princeton in 1914 is in my study, another token, like his father's goblet for wrestling, of talents that I so faintly inherited. When I notice it out of the corner of my eye, I feel what children of the famous must feel when they want to be or do or have something beyond their grasp.

In November 1942, Gouv wrote me from Naval Training School in Quonset, Rhode Island, where he'd been assigned after persuading the Navy to take him back, and said: "You must write and tell me how school, athletics and everything go with you." The following spring I was able to write him what he called "a nice long letter" inspired by my good performance at a school track meet: "How I wish I could have been at the field day," he said. "You really went to town and then some." What I had done now mostly escapes me, although I think I ran anchor on a relay team that won by the slightest of margins, but this was my last triumph on the playing field. My school reports from those early years surprise me because they credit me with athletic talent. The competition must have been negligible. In boarding school I had a whole catalog of sports I wanted to be better at–football, hockey, baseball, squash, high jumping, all activities that conferred prestige as soc-

1.

2.

3.

1.
John Murray Carnochan, aged nineteen, 1836, oil on canvas, signed "Powell"

2.
Mrs. John Carnochan and her children; the boy, standing, is John Murray Carnochan, ca. 1825, oil on canvas, attributed to Thomas Sully

3.
John Murray Carnochan, 1856, reproduction of original Ambrotype.

4.

5.

6.

4.
George Bliss, ca. 1885, studio photo,
W. H. Baker, NYC

5.
Walter Bliss, ca. 1922

6.
Walter Bliss's steam yacht *May*,
ca. 1911

7.
Rear lawn of Gov. Baldwin's home,
Fort Street, Detroit, ca. 1875

8.
Planting a tree, Wendover, ca. 1903

7.

8.

9.   10.   11.

9.
Henry Porter Baldwin, aged 37, 1851, studio photo, Randall, Detroit

10.
Henry Porter Baldwin, Governor of Michigan, ca. 1870, studio photo, C. C. Randall, Detroit

11. Henry Porter Baldwin, dressed for travel with umbrella, cane, and travelling bag, ca. 1885, studio photo, G. Grelling, "Artist," Detroit

12.
Katharine Baldwin Bliss as a child, ca. 1875

13.
Katharine Baldwin Bliss at Wendover with her daughters Ruth, Katharine, and Sibyll, ca. 1908

12.

13.

14.   15.   18.

16.   17.

14.
Mattie Goodridge Carnochan with roses, 1890s, studio photo, Davis & Sanford, NYC.

15.
Estelle Morris Carnochan in her wedding dress, 1856, reproduction of original Daguerreotype.

16.
Mattie Goodridge Carnochan, dressed for the Bradley Martin Ball, 1897, pastel on paper, J. Wells Champney

17.
Brevet Major General William W. Morris, ca. 1862, oil on canvas, signed, "Bandman"

18.
Gouverneur Morris Carnochan I, as an officer in the 7th Regiment, New York National Guard, ca., 1904, studio photo, Alman & Co., NYC

19.

21.

20.

19.
Sibyll Bliss Carnochan as a young
woman, ca. 1920

20.
Gouverneur Morris Carnochan II
in uniform, ca. 1943

21.
Gouverneur Morris Carnochan III
in uniform, ca. 1943

22.

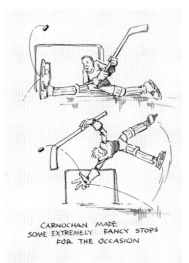

22.
"The Joy of Flying", ca. 1919,
photo by GM Carnochan II

23.
Cartoon of Gouverneur Morris
Carnochan II as Harvard goalie in
the 1914 Harvard-Princeton game,
unidentified Boston newspaper.

23.

cer and tennis did not. The Rector of the school even wrote a firm letter to students indicating that football was the manly thing to do and soccer wasn't. Tennis, equally hard to believe in these days of Sampras and the rest, was for sissies in white shorts (we'd all heard about Bill Tilden, and the school's most outright homosexual played tennis in the spring, not baseball). Especially I would have liked to be good at hockey, not only because my father had been but because the school team played a December game each year in old Madison Square Garden that I'd love to have taken part in, because the team's white and maroon uniforms were elegant, and because I liked playing the game, especially defense; skating backward and banging opponents into the boards were more satisfying than skating forward and trying to score goals, an attitude that, metaphorically speaking, has stayed with me. But I never got beyond the level of a second club team, a long way from Madison Square Garden. In college I was a mediocre high jumper as a freshman–very mediocre, for I never managed to jump higher than 5'4", using an already old-fashioned scissors kick, a height that can best be understood by knowing that the world's record in 1999 is over eight feet and that, at a paralympic games, a one-legged Chinese high jumper cleared 6'3". This was my entire athletic career at Harvard. And at New College, Oxford, where as a tall American I was granted the presumption of some ability in an eight-oared crew (at least in the middle of the boat where real skill counts less), I envied the talents of those who rowed not just for the college but for the university or who, as members of the Leander Club, a shrine of rowing, had the good fortune to wear pink scarves and caps and, if I remember right, pink socks too. Later on I yearned and still do to be better at tennis and at riding.

In all these sports I reached a level of competence above that of humiliation, good enough for the middle of the boat, but others defeated me utterly: skiing and golf in particular, both of which produced a sense of inadequacy equal to that produced by dancing, another activity, as *The Brooklyn Eagle* pointed out and as I had not known until I read the clipping, that my father was good at and one at which I feel most conspicuously inept, not least because my first wife, Nancy, was a good dancer, because my second wife, Brigitte, had the chance when young, though her mother would have none of it, to do ballet professionally, and because dancing is something you can never expunge from life so radically as skiing or golf. (Do you dance with the woman next to you at dinner? If not, why not? And if you do, what do you say when the band decides to play a waltz, something I have never been able to figure out at all?) My brother's advice about learning to dance had been quite right, if only I could have acted on it. But dancing is a good way to make a fool of yourself if you aren't proficient, as are skiing and golf: in skiing, you end up in a snowdrift; in golf, you tee off while others watch and if you slice or hook or flub the shot or, worst of all, miss the little dimpled white ball entirely, you feel the stifled amusement of the lookers-on. In both sports, before I gave them up as expensive lost causes, I sank to the level of stark humiliation.

In college, in the midst of an affair that was running a bumpy course, my girlfriend Cassie, a troubled and feral young woman with lots of money and a kinship with the Mellons, decided we should go skiing in Vermont. It was the thing to do and everybody did it, but my only previous experience was on a little hill at Wendover that I could negotiate by simply pointing the skis downward. This did not prepare me for mountains. Cassie, however, was a good athlete and an accomplished skier who had a cavalier attitude to the niceties of our relationship. I doubt we called it "going steady," a locution more in use among high schoolers than Harvard's aspiring sophisticates, and it would have been a misnomer: she was not steady, and the inequality of our skills on snow was a recipe for disaster. While I stuck to the snow-bunny slopes, she went flying down the advanced runs, usually pursued by one or another advanced and flying male. Eventually I tired of this and found a better way to spend my time when our car had a flat tire. My mechanical aptitude is no greater than my aptitude for skiing, but changing a tire had the advantage of attracting no spectators. Huddled on the snowy Vermont road, I found refuge from exposure on the mountain. After that I left the slopes in favor of reading in the cabin and pretending I was in the library.

Golf was even worse on one notable occasion. A year or so after college I was visiting my wife-to-be, Nancy, at her beach house on Cape Cod and her father, known as "Goody," asked me to play golf with him "at the club." He was president of a valve company in Springfield, Massachusetts, and convivial to a fault. I had no choice. At the club young boys from Dorchester took summer jobs as caddies and wore smart little uniforms that probably tried them sorely. They were very polite though they must have amused one another with tales of their

customers' adventures in the rough. After the usual ragged performance on the first few holes, I found myself surprisingly well placed on
a fairway. The caddies were 100 yards further along. I took an iron and
aimed for the green, only to hit not the high parabolic arch of a shot
that, when nicely executed, gives golf its peculiar beauty but a vicious
low liner that slammed into the shin of one of the caddies. I was sure
I'd broken his leg. Mercifully, I hadn't, and he continued gamely
through the rest of a round that must have been painful for him and
was excruciating for me. "Goody" seemed to take it all in stride, which
was gallant of him. How large a tip he gave the caddy I don't know but
enough to avert in those more innocent days any claims of injury and
suffering. When we went back to the old Victorian summer house on
the beach, I put on a bathing suit and plunged into the ocean to wash
away the awful memory. In the few rounds of golf I attempted after that
before giving up the game entirely, the shadow of that moment went
along with me like an incubus.

What I lacked in talent and however little I could add to the athletic
reputation of the Carnochans, I made up for, like millions of others,
in the intensities of being a fan and the more detached and tranquil lux-
uries of being a spectator. I can name the season and the year, if not
quite the day, when I became a fan, and I know who it was who changed
my life. On an early spring afternoon in 1939 when I was eight, I turned
on the radio I'd been given for Christmas and, switching from
station to station, stopped when I heard for the first of many times the
gentle southern tones of Red Barber broadcasting a Dodgers game.
It was only a spring training game, but I didn't know that because I
didn't know what spring training was. Barber's voice was to become
my solace, so comforting in its assurance, however dire the accidents of
a game (Mickey Owen's passed ball in the 1941 World Series),
however distressing when the Dodgers blew a ten-and-a-half-game
August lead over the Cardinals in 1942, however damaged the sport
with so many of its players gone to war, and despite the double
intrusion of death that broke up my small world, that nonetheless
everything remained somehow for the best. Only recently, looking
through an illustrated history of baseball and seeing a photograph
of Barber, I realized he bore a passing resemblance to my father.

But Red Barber was no Pangloss. He knew (you could tell) the meaning of pain, but in the soft presence of his voice, his vernacular celebra-

tion of "rhubarbs" and "catbird seats," you could accept the worst the game or the world had to offer. Being a fan meant listening to him during humid summer days on the porch of Wendover, and I was less alert when he handed over the microphone for two innings of each game to someone else. For me, Barber was an angel of light, and the Dodgers basked in his illumination; angels of darkness were Mel Allen of the Yankees and, later, Russ Hodges of the Giants, both of them shouters and screamers. When Russ Hodges, in 1951, howled over and over, "the Giants win the pennant, the Giants win the pennant, the Giants win the pennant," after Bobby Thomson hit the most famous home run in history, I could gladly have killed him. (When I met Bobby Thomson's very nice daughter years later at Stanford, I managed to muffle the sharpness of the memory.) And when the Dodgers beat the Yankees in four games in the 1963 World Series, led by the ravishing pitching of Sandy Koufax, I experienced waves of joy when I heard Mel Allen choked up and crying. (Or did I just imagine it?) Serves him right, I thought, but Red Barber would have been more magnanimous.

For all the rewards of listening to Barber and the Dodgers and later seeing the team play, being a Dodgers fan had its frustrations. If not so acute as those of Boston Red Sox fans, whose team has not won a World Series since 1918, suffering for eighty years the curse incurred for having sold Babe Ruth to the Yankees, they were painful nonetheless. Not only did I endure what every Dodgers fan had to, the failure of a great team, "the boys of summer," to win the World Series until the spell was broken in 1955, but I often had to root for them in unpleasant circumstances, being often in the wrong place in the wrong town, an outsider among fans from whom I had to guard my feelings. Except on the porch at Wendover, where I was alone with a mid-afternoon ginger ale and a three-decker peanut butter sandwich constructed from a loaf of unsliced bread, I was outnumbered, usually two or three or five or ten to one, by Giants fans around me. Growing up in Manhattan, I should by rights have been a Giants fan (no one I knew was a Yankee fan) but for the accident of tuning in to Red Barber in 1939. And, as if to make up for that happy accident and its subsequent joys, I had an equal number of grievous moments, of which the indelible worst was Thomson's home run. Not only did the Dodgers lose dreadfully, not only did I have to listen to Russ Hodges shrieking his triumph, but I watched the game on television with a roomful of college classmates who yelled and cheered and were as happy as Hodges about the outcome. There was nothing to do but slink inconspicuously out of sight and, next day, try to avoid the appearance of having been inconsolably wounded.

When I learned the Dodgers were moving to Los Angeles in 1958, I felt as if a burden had been lifted. Far from feeling betrayed, the normal reaction of Brooklynites, one of whom years later called Hitler, Stalin, and Walter O'Malley, the owner of the Dodgers who decided to go west, the three most evil men of the century, I looked forward to life without a fan's obsession, being 3,000 miles from its source. But only two years later I drove to San Francisco and my new job at Stanford and, coming over a rise in the road past Sacramento, I spun the radio dial: there was Hodges broadcasting a Giants game. The team had moved to San Francisco when the Dodgers moved to Los Angeles, and it hadn't hit me that coming to Stanford would mean I'd be surrounded again by the enemy. But that is what happened. For many an academic male, baseball is *the* sport, with its seductive mixture of strange and fatal chances on the one hand and minute statistical rigor on the other. The Stanford English department was a hotbed of Giants fans. When we went to ball games together, I always pretended it was only a game, that the outcome didn't matter much, that really I didn't care if the Dodgers lost. It was a lie. At such moments I felt about those nice people, good friends all, as I had about Russ Hodges in 1951; I could have killed them without compunction, especially when one of them would implore the Giants' pitcher to "stick it in his ear." Like Jonathan Swift, then the center of my other life as a scholar, I was out of place again: I told students that being Anglo-Irish, for Swift, was always to be in the wrong country, an Irishman in England, an Englishman in Ireland–like a Dodgers fan in Manhattan or in San Francisco.

By the 1960s Red Barber was no longer broadcasting, but Vin Scully was a good substitute, having learned his trade as Barber's apprentice. The only trouble was, Los Angeles was 400 miles away, picking up the broadcast was difficult, and even when the Dodgers played the Giants, I preferred to listen to Scully rather than Hodges. Many a night I hunched over a radio and strained to hear. The signal came in as dark fell and remained audible for a few hours, usually long enough for the game to reach an outcome though sometimes fading into obscurity as something crucial was happening or was about to. Sandy Koufax, however, had the virtue not only of pitching with exquisite skill but also of pitching as though he wanted to get off the field as fast as possible. So I heard all of his perfect game against the Cubs in late summer 1965–his fourth no-hitter–and without recourse to the car radio, which could be counted on for better reception than indoors. I know of another Dodgers fan, a poet, who not only listened regularly to his faraway team in his car but once, when the team lost, smashed its radio to bits. The usual lyric evocation of elysian fields misses the fact that baseball's pastures are often greenest in the mind's eye because being a fan is for many not mostly a matter of seeing games but listening to them. I find listening to them (and also watching them on the television screen) more intensely nerve-wracking than being there. Barber's great talent (and Scully's too) was to create in a way that the screamers can't the awful tension, even though in the long run he managed to assuage it also: because the world he saw was a friendly one, he treated the game not with intense partisanship as Hodges did but with mellow appreciation. Winning and losing were both important and also not the only thing that mattered when the game was over. I recognize Barber now as an ironist and credit him with teaching me more than just the game of baseball.

If being a fan is a mixture of blessings and torments, being a spectator has less complicated rewards, sometimes approaching rapture if the event is enhanced by the setting or if it makes history or simply if it is beautiful. Barber's skill was to unite all the blessings and torments of fandom with the quieter aesthetics of spectatorship. He taught me not to scorn spectatorship, and I have often been lucky being a spectator rather than a fan.

Once I snuck out of an academic conference, thereby missing a paper being given by an old antagonist, to my considerable but dissembled pleasure, so as to see the All-Blacks, New Zealand's national rugby team, play Australia in a tiny stadium in Dunedin, as near the South Pole as you can get and still be at an academic conference. The gaiety of playing hooky combined with delight in the remote intimacy of the place. I think Australia won, disappointing the home crowd, but I could be wrong: the outcome didn't matter so much as just being there. I went back to the conference and behaved myself after that.

Another time, in the company of a classicist friend from Antigua who followed West Indian cricket with the same passion as the Dodgers evoked in me, I applauded as the West Indians thrashed England at

Lord's and discovered in that famous ground what I thought made cricket a great game. If you bat only once or twice in a match and your score can range from no runs to hundreds, every time the ball is bowled the stakes are very high: complaints that cricket is tediously slow are off the mark, for the slowness gives the game its tensile strength, just as in baseball the batter's self-consciously deliberate march to the plate draws out the sense of embryonic destiny. That the West Indies won so handsomely was gratifying. If you don't come from Australia or New Zealand, there is little to choose emotionally in a rugby game between the two countries, unless perhaps that New Zealand is smaller and can play David to the Australian Goliath. But the politics of cricket are those of the colonial underdog rising up and smiting the master, a politics I find hard to resist. Mostly a spectator at Lord's, I was also something of a fan, applauding when my friend Gregson did even though I wasn't always sure why. If the West Indies had lost, however– it would have been hard for them to do, given the disparity between their talent and England's–I still would have rejoiced as I had in Dunedin at simply being there, not fully understanding all I was seeing but knowing I was on sacred ground.

Of all the rugby players in New Zealand and the cricketers at Lord's only one stays in mind, the West Indian fast bowler Marshall whose flash and style set him apart even to the neophyte spectator's eye. But often the athlete-hero, successor to the warrior hero, captures the imagination so vividly that being there matters. As a fan, you can watch television and see the game better than in the park. As a spectator you need to see the hero in the flesh not as an image in a box. When I was very young, I saw Cornelius Warmerdam in Madison Square Garden not long after he became the first to catapult himself over fifteen feet with the stiff wooden pole used in the days before fiberglass. I saw Maurice Richard, "the rocket," play hockey for the Canadiens against the Rangers in Madison Square Garden. In San Francisco I saw the in-comparable Brazilian soccer player Pele, though past his prime, on one of his numerous farewell tours. I saw Greg Louganis diving in the 1984 Olympics, a miracle of grace and control, as much remembered now for the accident that later almost killed him and posed the moral drama of his HIV-infected blood spilling in the water as for his extraordinary skill. But my greatest luck was being at two individual performances thirty years and six thousand miles apart.

The first was in 1954. I was a student, though not studying much, at New College, and one spring afternoon the crew practiced downriver at Henley, some miles from Oxford. We knew a race was scheduled for late in the day at Iffley track. Practice having ended, several of us jammed into the little coxswain's little Morris Minor and headed back toward Oxford. But the coxswain, though forever urging us on through the water, was a different being on dry land. We proceeded at a hideously slow pace, all the while imploring him to hurry up. He would respond grudgingly, briefly, then revert to his snail-like ways. We kept imploring. Time passed. The moment when the race was to begin passed. We arrived at Iffley. And there, from behind a chain link fence, at some distance above the track, I saw, more or less, the last lap of Roger Bannister's four-minute mile. That we missed three-quarters of the race didn't matter for we saw it as it turned into history. More than thirty years later I invited Bannister to speak at a Stanford conference on the culture of sports. He had been in an automobile accident some time before and walked haltingly. I was happy to tell him I'd seen him run on that famous day at Iffley.

The second performance that stays as sharply in mind is Reiner Klimke riding his Westphalian gelding Ahlerich to the gold medal in dressage at Los Angeles in 1984. Everybody who knows anything about sports knows about Bannister's mile, but not many in this country know about Klimke because dressage is unfamiliar except to a few and because its fine points can be all but indecipherable. Having ridden dressage tests, as they are called, at an elementary level and watched many more at an advanced level, I still have only the barest understanding of what judges actually see and judge when they assign scores to the more complicated individual movements with the arcane names: piaffe, passage, half-pass, flying changes. Even so, anyone who saw Klimke's ride in Los Angeles understood that it was special–though also beyond the reach of narrative, depending on a beauty beyond description. Bannister's mile in some measure belongs to everybody, not just the few hundreds who were present, because Bannister hitting the tape, blond hair flying, is a picture we know. Klimke's performance belongs to those who saw it and can re-create it in the mind's eye, see on the retina of memory his insouciant victory ride with flying changes at every stride, remember the applause. After he had won, Klimke said, "I'll never have another horse like Ahlerich." He had been riding for many years and knew that not only do horses like Ahlerich not come along often but that one Ahlerich in a lifetime is all you can hope for without hoping for more than your share. Since 1984 Klimke has not had another Ahlerich, though I saw him a few years ago riding a good Russian stallion, his hopes no doubt on the rise.

Achievement and loss are reciprocal, quantities that make a unity if multiplied together:"I'll never have another horse like Ahlerich." Samuel Johnson said we go from hope to hope, not satisfaction to satisfaction, but one hopes for a time when the satisfaction of not hoping for too much supplants the restless fever of wanting always more. Sport trades in endings. Even though we share (Johnson again) a "secret horror of the last," the last inning or the last period or the last quarter or the last move of the game happens over and over every day, as if to mimic the rhythm of daylight turning to dark and to domesticate any horror of the last. Comparing the different worlds of Anglo-Ireland and of England, Elizabeth Bowen said that "sport and death are the two great socializing factors in Ireland." I think she means the socializing between different social classes, between gentry and farmers, that happens at hunt meets and at wakes. I also think she has noticed that sport is entangled with premonitions of death. Those who cherish sport, whether players or spectators, can forget mortality in the exhilarations of the game but face it in the moment of victory or loss. Much is said of baseball's unique relation to the temporal: any baseball game, being unbounded by time, could go on forever but of course never does. And baseball, by now famously, is a field of dreams: if you build it, ghosts of the past will come through the green corn to play again. But any sport that results in someone winning, someone losing, is a matter of living and dying, not metaphorically unlike bullfights or any blood sport. When someone is badly hurt on a sports field, the crowd goes deathly quiet, knowing that sometimes paths of glory lead to the grave sooner rather than later. On the opening day of the 1996 baseball season, the plate umpire John McSherry called time "for a second" after the seventh pitch of the game, walked away from the plate, then collapsed and died of cardiac arrest before thousands of spectators. The newspapers carried pictures of him lying dead on the ground. The game was canceled, though some thought it should have gone on.

The entanglements of death and sport have allured poets since Pindar. Housman celebrated the athlete dying young:

The time you won your town the race
We chaired you through the market-place;
Man and boy stood cheering by,
And home we brought you shoulder-high.

To-day, the road all runners come,
Shoulder-high we bring you home,
And set you at your threshold down,
Townsman of a stiller town.

Too sententious, no doubt, for many tastes, including those who cherish the mock-heroic more than the heroic and see in the athlete-hero a substitute, however glamorous, for the real heroic thing. But the athlete as civic hero who wins the race for his town, then to become the townsman of death's quiet precincts, still has the power to move us. The civic meanings of sport have been lost increasingly to free agency–not just the player's right to sign up for as much money as the market-place affords but, along with it, the impermanence of civic allegiance. The Dodgers move to Los Angeles and forty years later are sold to Rupert Murdoch, the Giants move to San Francisco, the Boston Braves move to Milwaukee and then to Atlanta, the Quebec Nordiques of the National Hockey League become the Colorado Avalanche, the Minneapolis Stars go to Dallas (of all surprising places for a hockey team, except that now the Winnipeg Jets have moved and become, even more oddly, the Phoenix Coyotes). On and on it goes, but not without our having lost something of value.

Metaphors of sport litter our thinking about mortality and its meanings. Thomas Gray, seeing in his mind's eye boys on the playing fields of Eton and thinking of their momentary bliss, thought also of what lay ahead:"Regardless of their doom, the little victims play." We are victims in some cruel game of malignant gods–"merely the stars' tennis balls, struck and banded/ Which way please them," says the villainous Bosola in Webster's *The Duchess of Malfi*. And then there is Lear:"As flies to wanton boys are we to th' gods./ They kill us for their sport." Aberrations from the normal are called sports of nature, "lusus naturae." Yet sports are a joy and a consolation.

My passion for baseball has waned but not been extinguished. At the start of the 1996 season the Dodgers seemed to have their best team in years. Once again I found myself studying the box scores. A month or so into the season, this team of high promise had won twelve and lost fourteen. One evening I turned on the television and found them leading Florida 4-1 in the seventh. A Florida runner was on first base. Dodger pitchers quickly gave up two singles and a home run: Florida 5, Dodgers 4. I hurled a slipper (very soft, not likely to do harm) at the television and turned it off. The next morning I read that 5-4 had been the final score. It was an omen portending the sad end of a season in which the Dodgers lost their last three games to San Diego, fell out of first place, and as a "wild card" team lost three straight to the Braves in the playoffs. In 1997, they started the season badly, eventually recovered, and took the division lead from the Giants, only to lose it and finish a disappointing second. In 1998 they lost the first four games of the season in a row, their worst start in eleven years, and never recovered. Still, hope flickers and I wouldn't mind having one more good World Series to suffer through, say the Dodgers over the Yankees in six or seven, just like 1955. Whether I'd be able to watch a seventh game is something else again. It would be bearable, though, if the Dodgers scored ten or twelve runs in the first inning.

Sun and Summer Grass

Winters meant cold and cold was supposed to be good for you. It wasn't the fierce blue cold of the plains that can freeze your eyelids shut in bad winters but the raw edgy cold of Manhattan until I was thirteen, of the New Hampshire countryside until I was eighteen, of Harvard Yard until I was twenty-nine, except for a year of Oxford cold when I was twenty-three. They all had chilly places that stick in bone and memory: the cross streets of Manhattan when March winds blew in gusty currents off the rivers to the east and west; the skate house at boarding school where boys eager or reluctant got ready for the ice (and where, after coming off the ice one especially cold day, my pee was blue); the granite steps of Widener Library where students held on tight to the railing of wooden stairs installed over the stone at the first sign of winter and, having achieved the summit, entered the sanctuary to a blast of ill-regulated hot air; and, in Oxford, coldest of them all in the winter of 1954, a set of rooms previously occupied by a classics don, with an enormously high ceiling, two bedrooms, and, the only heat, a tiny gas fire where I and my roommate, a mild-mannered physicist and Rhodes Scholar from Austin who one day let me know, to my sorrow, that I had made him too well aware of the differences between us in class and wealth and who later died when a lunatic gunman began firing from the University of Texas campanile, would huddle and warm our hands. In Oxford my dark-eyed, gentle friend Fran, who's now a novelist and still a friend, would sometimes have tea or an Indian dinner with me, cordials against the chill of the air and the self-enforced chill of my own unconsummated feelings. (Whether they were her feelings, too, I never have asked but often wondered; on a mild summer afternoon the day before I returned to America, we watched tennis at Wimbledon, then kissed a long good-bye in the evening outside her flat in Fulham.) Also in Oxford there were early morning outings of the New College crew in winter, all of us in sweatshirts and shorts, after ice-breakers had done their job so cargo could get through the locks and freezing oarsmen could answer the coxswain's insistent "stroke, stroke, stroke." Bracing and northern, cold was good for you because it was an antidote to tropical, or for that matter Californian, indolence. In the 1960s the English Department at Cornell, recruiting a young member of the Stanford faculty, told him that in Ithaca's dreadful climate he would get some work done but in California he would come to an unproductive end. He went to Cornell, then later to Harvard, so perhaps the cold weather theory has something to it. New Englanders and other lovers of the cold think it builds character. That is another reason why Uncle Fred, spending all those years in the African heat, seemed to my cold-weather self a surprising case.

During summer vacations from college, I could appreciate the cold-weather myth, for I often sweltered helplessly in cars of the Lackawanna railroad that had sat in the Hoboken sun for hours, ready to carry commuters back to Basking Ridge or Far Hills or Peapack or, in my case, the more prosaic Bernardsville. But the summers I spent in banks, brokerage houses, publishing companies, and boiling commuter trains weren't real summers, not compared to those shimmering days earlier before conscience and my mother's lack of income made me think I had to earn a fragment of a living and help pay the Harvard bills, days when, left to myself with Wendover's several hundred acres as my private if decaying demesne, I could do whatever fancy inspired, alone in the warmth of summer and little heeding, until the katydids began their nightly racket in August, the cold that was to come.

Though it took much away, the war also had some welcome side effects: because gasoline was rationed, a few gallons a week, obligations like having to mingle with other children were mostly canceled. I was comfortable with wintertime schoolmates, but summer playmates and summer parties, arranged by somebody's mother and agreed to, on my behalf, by mine, were hard going, and although I managed to improve on one early performance when, aged perhaps five, I spent all of someone's birthday party in a corner as far away as possible from the action, I never achieved any social ease, preferring to this day the solitude of the library or the quiet camaraderie of the tennis court to the enforced conviviality of social gatherings. Other obligations like going to the Lake Club for swimming lessons also mercifully ceased with the war. I had hated the cold water, the nasty bottom, the dank wet smell of the open roomful of canoes, the eager instructors, and the children who were better swimmers than I. On mornings when lessons were scheduled, I looked hopefully out the windows of the big brick house and prayed for rain, the more the better, so I would be spared. Wartime eliminated the need for divine intervention, and lessons having stopped, I could spend those mornings and days as I chose.

Best of all were the trees to be climbed, thousands of them (I had begun climbing as soon as I reached an age when I could escape the watchful eye of my nurse), maples, apple trees (almost but not quite too old to bear fruit in the autumn), a mulberry (where my Irish terrier treed a groundhog and I, boyishly and cruelly, shook it to the ground for the terrier to finish off), a copper beech, a grove of pines, a Japanese maple with its tracery of deep red leaves (smaller than ordinary maples but with a few branches you could stand on), a great horse chestnut lucky to have escaped the blight that killed many of its kind. Other trees, unscalable, I looked at longingly: the elms, whose lowest branches were ten feet off the ground; an exotic gingko; and the utterly-out-of-reach arboreal Everest of Wendover forest, a giant locust tree next to the porch steps leading down to the sloping lawn that looked out to the hills beyond. Walter Bliss had planted many of the trees in 1903 and 1904 as the house was being built on what had been the mostly bare top of Bernardsville "mountain." With great labor and expense the trees were brought up the hill on horse-drawn wagons. Sitting on top of this panoramic world, I wanted to get still higher above it, there to command, from maple or pine or mulberry, a prospect of the lavish countryside. The trees were ladders of the imagination and when, from a window halfway up the stairs, I watched the giant locust swoop and sway in the 1938 hurricane and finally fall to earth with a terrific crash, luckily away from rather than towards the house, I was bereaved. Ginger ale was ordered from the pantry as a comfort.

Not only were there trees and other high birdlike perches, there were also secret coverts to hide away in. My favorite was a thicket of honeysuckle, tucked away near an old greenhouse, that made a canopy almost impervious to light and into which I could creep, there to find a dark theater of shadows and half lights, a cave like Plato's (which, when I eventually learned about it, seemed an enchanting place, no matter what Plato may have thought). Later I wrote a book about eighteenth-century thought and literature called *Confinement and Flight*. It was filled with prisons and islands and secret gardens, on the one hand, and panoramas, prospects, and high-flying air balloons, on the other. Walter Bliss thought he was building a country estate with a Big House, as they are called in Ireland, for the ages. What he gave me was a world of ecstatic enclosures and views from the heights where solitariness enhanced the vividness of everyday.

It was also a world full of small and mostly flying things that seized my imagination. With a mind more like Uncle Fred's, I might have found in them inspiration for a different vocation. Scientists like E. O. Wilson and William Hamilton were captivated early by ants and beetles (and Wilson also by snakes) and went on to turn their infatuation into evolutionary biology. Before he went to Africa, Uncle Fred not only studied and published articles on a family of beetles but also formed what his uncle, recommending him to the Explorers Club, called the largest collection of coleoptera in the country. Myself, I doted on ladybugs perched on a leaf's edge and dragonflies that skimmed the top of the low circular pool full of water lilies, loved gathering the dried, discarded skins shed by cicadas, and admired the sheen of Japanese beetles as I flicked them into turpentine–an occupation for which my grandmother paid me a nickel a corpse and my aunt Priscilla, who lived in a house on the property while her husband, Bill, was away at war, paid me less lavishly, indeed I thought downright stingily, just a penny. On days after it rained the damp brought out myriads of snails on the long, curving wall of irregular stones beside the almost mile-long driveway to the Big House, and they charmed me nearly as much as the denizens of the air. Best of all were the hundreds of fireflies at evening, so easy to capture in the cup of my hand and put in a jar to display their incandescent beauty before I set them free again. I wondered how fireflies made their fire, but mostly the natural world seemed not to need an explanation; it was just there–and beautiful, even the Japanese beetles whose devouring habits and oriental origin made them enemy number one in the insect world, even the snails whose slimy trails turned shimmering and crystalline when they dried. It was people, especially grown-ups, that needed explaining: ladybugs and dragonflies and cicadas didn't need to be roped into a system of understanding.

If the natural world of the Wendover landscape was thriving, its human world was sadly frayed: of all the buildings and barns, none but the Big House and a greenhouse with some broken panes yet still hot and fragrant- the greenhouse that stood beside the honeysuckle cave–served their original purpose, the others being in various stages of disuse or dereliction. The stables had no horses in them, the brood barn no mares, the cow barn no cows, the chicken house no chickens, the pig house no pigs, the ice house no ice, the hay barn no hay, and the "boarding house," standing like an isolation ward at the farthest reach of the property, no workers.

When the war ended and Priscilla's husband came home, the two of them, childless, made an effort to bring things back, not to where they had been but at least to the condition of a working dairy farm. Cows were again in their stanchions, chickens in their nests, baled hay in the lofts–though pigs never returned to the pig house. These efforts made only brief and modest headway, however, against the tides of decline, and when Uncle Bill became seriously allergic to cows, the dream of paradise regained was set back, as if some higher force resisted any restoration. But in fact I cared only a little about live cows, and the chickens were always pecking at me when I reached under them to collect their eggs, so that my hands were often scraped and bloody from banging them against the edge of the metal nests when I tried to escape the attention of an angry hen. The disused and derelict structures on the landscape meant as much to me as the proud fiefdom in its glory days, with its prize cows, prize horses, prize chickens, and prize pigs, could ever have done. The deserted village was an endless source of alluring spaces: had I become an archaeologist, as I sometimes wish, I would have loved excavation. For one thing, it gets you outdoors while the seductions of the library, however powerful, are airless. For another thing, digging into the ancient ground yields actual scraps and shards, not just textual memories, of long-ago lives. As it was, I had to settle for writing a book about Edward Gibbon and his *Decline and Fall of the Roman Empire* to satisfy my *ruinenlust,* my lust for ruin.

Richest of Wendover's archaeological sites were the brick stables. Almost as much care had been lavished on them as on the Big House, and they were built on the same scale. There were two wings, one for horses and the other for carriages, a connecting area between the wings for grooming the horses, an office with cases of ribbons, a tack room, lofts, an open courtyard created by the three sections of the building and a high wall across the front split by an entrance more than big enough for carriages, and, off the central area at the back, a balcony with no functional purpose I could discover. The stables were as ugly as the house if less overwhelming, but they were a trove of treasure. By the 1930s, the grooming area had been converted to a garage (housing a Ford station wagon with real wood siding), the stalls were empty, the office disused and dusty, but the wing for carriages was another story. Like an eighteenth-century pharmacy I once saw preserved in Rome, or like artists' studios maintained as at the moment when their proprietor passed from the scene, the carriage house was a memorial to a departed way of life, the carriages still there in two facing rows, yearning to be driven. And there I was to fill the need. The pharmacy in Rome was kept up by a monastic order, perhaps the Benedictines. When I rang the doorbell, a decrepit monk opened the door and led Brigitte, by then my wife of several years, and me up the creaky stairs. I wondered if he ever resorted to leftover salves or tinctures or remnants of the eighteenth-century pharmacopoeia? Myself, I would have been tempted.

There were ten or twelve carriages left in the stables, from simple to grand, and a sleigh for wintertime. I think one of the carriages was called a training break and another a station wagon, no doubt for Walter Bliss to travel the five miles down Bernardsville mountain to the railroad station. But most alluring of all was the elegant coach for church-going and other formal occasions, with its glistening ebony and yellow exterior and its robber-baronial coat of arms on the side door that opened and shut with the quiet precision of the door on a Mercedes. On sunny weather days of the mind, you could be the driver. On wet weather days you could ride inside and luxuriate in soft gray plush. Had I been more precocious, what a spot the interior would have been for ardent romping. But if I'd been more precocious, I would not have spent so much time in these solitary and fictive activities. Romping would come later, much later than I would have liked.

Another missed opportunity for back-seat precocity was the 1921 Rolls-Royce, Walter Bliss's last present to Katharine before his early death, a sentimental memento, placed on blocks and filling up a whole corner of the carriage house diagonally opposite the ebony and yellow splendor of the old coach. In the back seat of the Rolls, as in the passengers' cabin of the coach, shades could be pulled down for a privacy that I never needed, but the driver's seat was so seductive in its mechanical ingenuities that, like Starship Enterprise, it was a good place to fantasize adulthood. I had no idea what the instruments were for that littered the environs of the steering wheel, but like the insect world they didn't need to be explained, and there they delightfully were to be turned or pushed or pulled. If the splendid old coach came from Edith Wharton's *fin de siècle*, the Rolls came from a few decades later, too proper and ponderous for Fitzgerald or Gatsby but with a touch, nonetheless, of their sojourn in the Long Island sun. Later on *The Age of Innocence* and *Gatsby* made me wonder what doings in the past might have touched this sphere of my innocence with some clandestine guilt or shame. What audacities might the Club-Fellow have been able to ferret out? But in childhood, innocence seemed all around. The boarding house, however, darkened the peaceful scene, even to young eyes.

The route from the stables to the boarding house, second only to the stables in archaeological interest, traversed the entire estate, and by bicycle (for as much of the voyage as a bicycle could manage) took twenty minutes or more: down the back driveway lined with tulip trees (no good for climbing) and meadows on either side, across the main driveway and its treacherous blue gravel on which I once crashed and scraped myself badly, down a hill to a lower road in the woods leading past a pump house from which came fresh and frigid blue water to the swimming pool after it had been emptied of water turning green with algae, out of the woods and through a file of maples (very good for climbing), past the brood barn with the handsome hackney stallion as a weather vane, lording it over all his mares (but now domesticated on the wall of my living room), down past the duck pond, up past the cow barn, down past the chicken house and the dairy, past the house where superintendents and foremen had lived–vacant until Aunt Priscilla and Uncle Bill remodeled it and moved in–and way down past the pig house where the road ran out and bicycling became impossible. From the pig house it was a short trek through the woods and the underbrush to the boarding house and its Faulknerian rot.

Unlike the stables, the boarding house contained only a few leftover artifacts: an occasional calendar tacked on a wall with a buxom, smiling blonde pinup girl left to look out on the desolate scene; some bureaus, some standing cupboards, pitchers for hot water and basins for shaving, some broken china. But the real allure was the ruin itself. Rank vegetation, vines and thistles and poison ivy, grew all around. I wondered who had lived there and what their lives, so different from mine, could have been like.

I worked summers on the quixotic dairy farm that Wendover became and got to know some laboring farmers and farm boys well enough to guess at the rough camaraderie of the boarding house. One old farmer, among the several hired by Bill and Priscilla, whose search for someone competent to manage the place was always coming up short, was a gap-toothed, tobacco-chewing old rascal, not at all like the Irish gardener who by my time was the only survivor of Wendover's old days, a deacon in the local church who radiated a leonine decorum, who never referred to the big brick house except as the Big House (to the irritation of my mother, who thought the name pretentious and didn't know that every big house in Ireland was a Big House), and who looked back to the old days of Wendover and of even grander estates where he had worked in Ireland, with barely articulate longing. The farmer was Alex. The Irish gardener was Matt. Alex was the real world, Matt was a dying species. Once, while we were loading some heavy bales of hay into a loft, Alex said to me, pointing to one of them, "That'll make you grunt at both ends, won't it?" I was shocked. I was also shocked, but didn't fall into the trap, when a local farm boy, working in the fields with me and a friend of his, said, "Bet you didn't know that if you masturbate you grow hair on the back of your fingers." "Oh?" I said, "hmmm," but didn't look at my hands. I thought the life of the boarding house must have been made up of moments like this–unless worse things went on there than I could guess at, just as worse things, for all I knew, may have gone on up the hill in the world of stately carriages and the Rolls-Royce. The boarding house, with its pinups and the thick vegetation crowding around, offered a glimpse of the underside of things and posed a hard threat to process in an adolescent imagination.

If the Wendover of my childhood was a deserted village, its only inhabitants a few day laborers, including a round old Italian named Mike and Matt the foreman-gardener, who had little to be foreman of and who chiefly loved the immense dahlias and gladioli that he grew and delivered daily in bunches to the Big House, the house and its staff were a better preserved version of what it had been like in earlier days. On the staff were West the butler, stately and balding, very English and very butler-proper; Johnson the plump, maternal, unmarried housekeeper; and a passing number of maids both upstairs and downstairs, one of whom gladdened a summer by her youth and prettiness and kindness when I sought her company in the pantry under cover of reading the sports pages of the *Daily News*, unacceptable tabloid fare in the region above stairs where the Republican proprieties of the *New York Herald Tribune* were unopposed except perhaps in my father's inner thoughts, for he was a Democrat who as a young newspaper publisher in Rockland County had supported Jim Farley, later Roosevelt's postmaster general and political advisor. Maybe the pretty maid's name was Maggie, very likely she was Irish, and to my eye she was utterly desirable in her starched black and white outfit: my heart beat a little faster as I pushed through the swinging door from the dining room into the breakfast room, then through another swinging door to the pantry, hoping to find her there. Had this been a French story, she would have taken me one day into a flowery bower and taught me what I wanted to learn. Eventually maybe we would have moved on to the cabin of the Sunday coach or the back seat of the Rolls. Even better, maybe I would have found my way to her room in the servants' quarters, off-limits to me, on the third floor. But the truth is that between Maggie (if that was her name) and me, nothing of interest, not an inquisitive glance, ever occurred. Probably I concerned her not at all.

I hardly know whether it was before Maggie or after that I first learned the rudiments of what I wanted to know in the way such things usually happened then, namely, amongst a group of nasty-minded boys.

In my case it was campers suffering a collective summer internment on Lake Winnipesaukee in the middle of New Hampshire, where my mother had insisted I go, maybe in the very hope that I'd learn something of what she and I, in each other's presence, not only didn't talk about but would have been hard-pressed even to concede its existence, namely, sex. On afternoon sails in small boats, one of the older boys took the tiller and would quiz his little crew to discover who knew what about which facts of life and to display his own superior knowledge. We didn't know much, and what I learned about masturbation was knowledge I could use. Puberty was long in coming, however, and I feared it might never, that I might always have the same squeaky voice but at last, near the stables, in high sun, as I lay hidden in the tall grass of summer, fulfillment arrived. Now my voice would change, now I would grow a beard, now–if only the chance were ever offered–I could do whatever it was that boys did to girls, or with them.

I was in college before that goal was achieved, awkwardly and somewhat ignominiously on the well-carpeted floor of a living room in the Dakota, 1 West 72nd Street, where Cassie's father lived–even then, years before John Lennon died there, one of the most glamorous apartments in Manhattan and, I suppose, one of the most glamorous places anywhere to get laid, especially for the first time. I didn't know the Dakota was famous, although I went to a party there at which were some famous or at least beautiful people including Elizabeth Montgomery, then very young, who sang Gershwin:"In time the Rockies may crumble/Gibraltar may tumble/(They're only made of clay)/But –our love is here to stay." Hearing the song, looking at the loveliness of lights in the park and over on the East Side where I lived, I thought that I too was in love forever. Still I'd rather have given up my virginity not in the Dakota but in the fields of Wendover. On a bright spring day, near the end of what had been a miserably unhappy affair (for me) instead of one for the ages, Cassie and I made love in the shade of a larch tree at the foot of Wendover's sweeping lawn. It was far nicer than the floor of the Dakota. The smells of mown grass and hay, of conifers and apple trees, mingled with the sweet acrid pungency of incipient life.

The larch tree stands now in the middle of the eighteenth fairway of Roxiticus Golf Club, which is what Wendover became after Katharine's death. The Big House is gone, burnt to the ground in a 1979 fire, the result of a failure in the ancient electrical system, that killed the manager of the club and his wife who had been asleep inside. Cassie died young, probably from alcohol and excess. But the tree survives. Robert Pack, who writes poems that I would like to have been able to write, has one called "The Trees Will Die." In it he hopes that perhaps the trees will not all have to die:

> When I consider how
> a man-made shift in climate of a few degrees
> reveals the rebel power we now
>
> have learned to cultivate
> in order to subdue the animals
> and take dominion, like a curse,
> over the fields, the forests, and the atmosphere–
> as if the universe
>
> belonged to us alone-I wonder
> if consideration of the family of trees
> might give us pause
> and let us once again obey the sun,
> whose light commands all human laws.

When I've gone back to see the Wendover landscape, now a palimpsest inscribed with faint markings of the past, it has always been at a time of year when golfers have been few so I could try to see and feel what was there then instead of what is there now. Once I talked to a lone golfer about to tee off on the eighteenth hole. He was surprised to learn I'd lived in the Big House that had been at the end of the fairway. But I did. And every so often a golf ball, hit not long but straight, must plunk itself down on the spot where desire, obeying the sun, once had its dominion.

Fair Harvard

The Carnochans went to Harvard, the first Gouverneur Morris Carnochan having graduated–in company with George Santayana–in 1896. His sons, Fred and Gouv, followed. And Gouv's son, also Gouv, was in the class of 1941, though he didn't do much work while he was there, was suspended after a year or two and, the war intervening, never came back. So I went to Harvard, too. Harvard's dean of admissions, said to be a stern New Englander, came to St. Paul's to interview candidates, but I thought his sternness was his way of letting us know he was doing us a favor by inviting us to Cambridge. For most of us the favor was not in any doubt.

Whether I would have been admitted now, who knows? The Sunday *New York Times Magazine* carried a story in April 1996, about four very good students from Van Nuys High School in Southern California. Each had applied to Harvard. One was admitted. Of the three who weren't, one was a young woman of Polish lineage, third in her class with grades of five (the highest score) on four advanced placement exams, and a speaker of Mandarin Chinese. A Harvard alumni interviewer ("the guy was 75," and "very uptight") asked what was special about her, she said she was studying Mandarin, and he said, perhaps not noticing that she wasn't Asian, "Oh, half the population of Harvard speaks Chinese. What else?" The one student who did get in was principal violinist in a community orchestra and won twenty-nine straight matches on her varsity tennis team. That her father was Mexican and Italian, her mother black and Native American, was a worry to the family: "I'm torn," her mother said. "I'm in favor of affirmative action, but Maya doesn't need it."

The year after I graduated a cable arrived at New College from Harvard's dean of freshmen, with the patrician name of F. Skiddy von Stade (he was an uncle or an older cousin of the singer Frederica von Stade, the Cherubino of everybody's dreams), asking if I would like to be one of his assistants, what Harvard called a baby dean. Though unprepared by experience or by temperament, I cabled back quickly, yes, and after I was on the job stole a look in the Registrar's files at my College Board scores, which were not then made public. I had done well on the verbal score and not badly on math. Like the Dodgers' Orel Hershiser (whom I saw beat the Mets to win the final game of the National League play-offs in 1988), I was good at Latin, having endured Caesar and Cicero (certainly the least promising way possible to introduce Latin to young students) and then having had a glimpse, in Virgil, of what the literature had to offer if given the chance. I had done some of the usual extracurricular things at St. Paul's. I had been news editor of the school paper, "published by the boys of St. Paul's School fourteen times a year" and called *The Pelican* because Christian symbolism adopted the fable that pelicans fed their young with their own blood. I had been an officer in one of the two debating societies (I remember their odd names—"Cadmean" and "Concordian"–but not which one I was in) and treasurer of something called (alas) the Missionary Society or (alas, again) the Mish. What the Missionary Society was and what its treasurer did, other than what treasurers normally do, I have no recall: the only reason I know I was treasurer is that I found the information in a school yearbook. Perhaps being a treasurer was part of my genetic inheritance from Walter Bliss. No doubt the Missionary Society did good works, and no doubt I've suppressed, in post-colonial times, the idea that I might ever have had a missionary instinct. I had had a minor role in a school play. I had been on the student council, not by election but, less prestigiously, by appointment. Athletically, I had little to offer; dramatically, very little for I never discovered what to do with my hands; musically, nothing whatsoever, for unlike my father, who had a fine tenor voice but whose genes seem to have gone mostly on vacation when my turn came to be born, I'm nearly tone deaf although I know now what I like: namely, almost anything composed before 1800, especially Monteverdi, Mozart, and Purcell's *Dido and Aeneas*, in which I can sometimes even recognize the use of the minor key without understanding what it really is.

But whatever I could or couldn't offer Harvard in 1949, my name was Carnochan, I was a "legacy," and that was enough to have gotten me in with even less on the record. Nowadays forty percent of legacies are admitted, so perhaps I'd still be among the chosen. If so, I'd be torn like Maya's mother wondering whether I'd have been accepted without the accident of having had a grandfather, a father, an uncle, and a brother who all went to Harvard.

In the fall of 1949, I took the same ten o'clock train from Grand Central Station to Boston as I had in St. Paul's days, got off four hours later in South Station, and took the subway to Harvard Square, emerging from the dim underground into the sharp September light. When I see freshmen arrive at Stanford accompanied by parents and siblings, I wonder if they are as anxious for their family to leave as I would have been if Sibyll hadn't let me go alone. I found my room easily. It was on the fourth floor of Straus Hall, steps from the Square, but having found it, I had little to do but unpack and wait for something to happen. More sophisticated classmates took their fake ID's to local pubs while I pored over Harvard's "Confidential Guide to Freshman Courses," otherwise known as the "Confy Guide," the entirely unconfidential booklet that evaluated freshman courses and sold everywhere for twenty-five cents. Samuel Beer's Social Sciences 2 got high marks: most students "raved about Beer as 'marvelous,' 'dynamic,' and 'inspiring'" though a few, who must have been terrible intellectual snobs, probably from Exeter, said that "he oversimplified." I. B. Cohen's Natural Sciences 3 was pegged as the perfect non-demanding course for non-scientists: "If you're scared of science and don't want to spend a year in technicalities and formulae, this historical approach is probably the best." I decided I'd take both Cohen and Beer.

Straus C-41 had a living room with dormer windows, two bedrooms looking out on the Square, and one other occupant, a plump and gloomy graduate of a local prep school who came from Boston's North Shore and who managed a sepulchral "hello." But he soon became a missing person, never showing up and not telling me where or how he spent his time. So I had the place to myself, as much as the acres of Wendover, and once again a high point of vantage to look out from–on the one side at the grim towers and brick of Matthews Hall, covered then with ivy that now is gone, like that on other buildings in the Yard, lest it have eaten them away; and on the other, at the subway kiosk, at Albiani's cafeteria, purveyor of junk food to hungry late-evening freshmen and ragged habitués of the Square, at a movie theater, a bank, and the Harvard Cooperative Society, always known as the Coop, never the Co-op. It was as if whoever assigned rooms to freshmen that year, a hateful job that was to be mine when I became a baby dean, had for once been blessed by chance. It would have gone against the social grain to have asked for a single room, which I wouldn't have been given anyway, but ending up in luxurious solitude, if sometimes and momentarily an ambiguous-seeming gift, was nonetheless the best thing I could have hoped for. In that room, I translated Horace, Catullus, and Lucretius for the kindly but as I later found out troubled and alcoholic Peter Elder, learned enough German to pass the Ph.D. reading exam (you could use a dictionary) some years later, encountered Aquinas and Freud in Beer's course and Heisenberg in Cohen's, and read every course assignment twice, a compulsive habit that saw me through Harvard with an academic record that I did everything I could to conceal because it would have been socially incriminating. I wrote a paper that first year on Lucretius and his version of the social contract, a purportedly learned performance though all its learning was borrowed from Beer's course, a paper that Elder, who himself suffered from writer's block, said should be published. I was pleased but knew the praise was probably undeserved.

The next three years were more gregarious. I lived in a room with three classmates from St. Paul's, a cliquish and snobby-seeming thing to do, but in my case and perhaps in theirs inspired by a lack of ease in making new friendships. One of us became a theatrical agent and later an expatriate in London–with many a scabrous tale of his famous clients and a gift for irreverence that has kept us close for nearly fifty years. Another, now dead, became an assistant to Henry Kissinger soon after graduation and eventually a professor of political science who wrote craggy books on subjects like Hegel and American religion. As an undergraduate he tried to write a musical, banging out melodies on an out-of-tune piano in our room (at least it sounded out of tune even to me when he played it, but perhaps that was because he had no formal musical training whatever). The last of our foursome became a successful architect, surprising to me given his passion for Gilbert and Sullivan, a taste I thought incompatible with any capacity for aesthetic understanding (in music I know what I don't like as well as what I do). The fact that Cassie carried him off for part of a weekend that supposedly belonged to me did not improve my opinion of him. After college we met only once, by chance, in Cambridge, and my opinion sank further still when he recalled, in the presence of my daughter Sarah who was with me, that he had once upon a time, so he made it seem, stolen my girlfriend when she in fact had stolen him. But he died not many years ago, and decency requires saying that he was a good as well as a successful architect.

I also joined a "final club," Harvard's version of fraternities but smaller, with peculiar names like the Porcellian and the Fly. This admission does not come easily: the clubs are usually defended on grounds that very few students belong to them and that therefore they don't disrupt the democratic values of the academic environment, an argument that deserves some sort of prize for sophistry. The hierarchic ranking of the clubs is firmly established: the Porcellian, most Bostonian of the lot, is on top and notable for, among other things, not having admitted

Franklin Roosevelt. The club I joined in the spring of sophomore year, having failed to make it on my first try after the endless series of fall drinking parties to estimate the sociability and suitability of candidates, was less prestigious than the Porcellian or the Fly, appealed to athletes who enjoyed sports like rugby, and had a marginally less funny name. But I was grateful for any social acceptance, belated or not. Looking back, I can't discover any redeeming purpose in the club's activities, which consisted mostly of drinking, playing pool, placing bets on horse races with the Irish steward who doubled as a bookie, and every so often–in the basement–watching badly made pornographic movies, described by the entrepreneurial club member who arranged for their showing as "the greatest show on earth." It was also in front of the Owl Club's television set that I sat and watched and suffered when Bobby Thomson hit his home run.

By the time I graduated, Harvard had gotten deep under my skin. When I watched the president-designate Nathan Pusey, a member of the twenty-fifth anniversary class, march in the graduation procession, I fantasized that twenty-five years later the new president-designate of Harvard just might happen to be me. A few years earlier my sister's husband had been installed as Episcopalian bishop of Western New York. I had been released from school to go to the ceremony and had read in the Buffalo paper the next day that Bishop Scaife had been the "cynosure" of all eyes. I had no idea what a cynosure was nor that "the cynosure of all eyes" was a cliché. It seemed quite grand, and I thought that being a cynosure of all eyes would be desirable, a misguided hope for someone whose anxieties in the face of the public world would prove almost intractable. Eventually I learned that "cynosure" had to do with the little dipper and the North star and meant, in Greek, dog's tail. Eventually I also learned that being the cynosure of all eyes as president of Harvard or president of anything was not a likely nor for me a desirable outcome. I had neither the stamina nor the thick skin nor the public agility required. The closest I ever came was being interviewed for a university presidency in the Southeast. I came away convinced that even if I were the trustees' choice, as seemed improbable, it was not for me. I withdrew politely. Impolitely, I invented a country –western song inspired by some of the university's trustees: its title, which I never got beyond, was "I'm just a hillbilly millionaire." University presidents nowadays get wagged by all the dogs they find themselves attached to. It's a job for the very strong or very masochistic. But in 1953 Nathan Pusey looked to me like the world's luckiest man, though events of his lackluster and ultimately troubled presidency were to make him seem otherwise.

The spell of Harvard lay in the rarity of some of its teachers, by whom I was captivated as I had been by Wendover's fields. To be sure, it had its dull pedagogues, too, one of them a wizened little Texan named Hyder Rollins, famous as an editor who ensured the perfection of his editions by reading proofs backwards, including all the punctuation marks, and in whose courses graduate students were required to read and comment on other graduate students' papers, having checked all their quotations for accuracy; we were Rollins's citation police. A story is told that catches his dry-as-dustiness: seeing a graduate student whom he knew on the steps of Widener Library, Rollins asked him in his Texas twang what his dissertation was going to be about. "I think maybe humor in Henry James," said the student, who later became a well-known critic. "Oh," said Rollins, "you Catholics always go back to Newman." (Rollins was a surprisingly intransigent atheist.) "No, sir," said the student, "I said 'humor in Henry James'." "Oh," said Rollins again, "I wondered what Newman had to do with it." But even Hyder Rollins had something superlative to be said for him: he was quite the dullest man I have ever known.

Other of Harvard's teachers, aware that they were or were on their way to being legends, were the source of undergraduate delight, if not necessarily reverence. I. B. Cohen's dandified watch fob, Sam Beer's suits, the medievalist B. J. Whiting's puckish jests, Adam Ulam's well-maintained Eastern European accent, these were antic foibles of exotic glamour. When Ulam called Maxim Karolik, the collector of American art who had married a very rich and much older woman, "a stahrrrving Moldahvian tenor," I savored every extra ripple of sound. If Whiting required in every exam he ever gave in his Chaucer class a knowledge of the seven deadly sins, he inspired in his students a variety of mnemonic devices—mine was PILEGAS = pride, ire, lechery, envy, greed or gluttony, avarice, sloth; a friend reports that his was PSGLEIA—and he provided us with information that in a lifetime we could never shake. If the redoubtable Sam Beer, later president of Americans for Democratic Action who in his fifties would take up sky-diving and make 199 recorded jumps, chose to wear the jacket of his wide blue pinstripe suit with the trousers of his wide brown pinstripe suit and the jacket of his wide brown pinstripe suit with the trousers of his blue one while discussing scholasticism or the French Revolution, well, he also introduced us to Ruth Benedict's *Patterns of Culture*, and Benedict taught us that different cultures have different values and that we should beware of normative assumptions. For a graduate of Buckley School and of haughty hockey-playing St. Paul's, going to Cambridge in 1949 was like an anthropological field trip to Fiji or to the Trobriand islands. And I liked the natives, almost all of them.

Of course they were all white males, but it didn't occur to me to be troubled about that. Nor, going on fifty years later, do I feel guilty for having enjoyed being in their presence, however exclusive their little society. The conventions that supported it are gone, and I prefer to sing its local color, however sometimes outrageous, and remember its virtues, whatever their limitations. For some of these white males made Harvard an oasis where I could drink in quietly, as if under cover of darkness, the values of the thoughtful life.

In my last three years, I lived by the Charles River in Eliot House, then the haven of clubmen, preppies, and genteel intellectuals, but home to a resident faculty of gifted eccentrics and also one young Canadian, in every respect but for the wartime accident of losing his right arm, the most resolutely normal-seeming of men–a substitute father to many of us, as he became to me. This was John Conway, dependable as Bunyan's Mr. Standfast or Melville's Starbuck and ever a counterweight to the gala flamboyance of his colleagues. But without its cast of eccentrics, Eliot House would have been a less heady place.

The most willful of them all was Arthur Darby Nock, author of the once-famous *Conversion* who at the extraordinary age of twenty became annual reviewer of the year's work in classical studies and then, late in his twenties, Harvard's Frothingham Professor of the History of Religion. Nock was an English eccentric of epic accomplishment. At one Christmas party in the Master's lodgings, he rushed from one person to another, introducing himself on the fly, even though everyone in the room knew who he was. "Hello," he would say, "I'm Nock, N for nuisance, O for obnoxious, C for cantankerous, and K for Ku Klux Klan." Then he would hustle off to try it on someone else. Another time, he learned from Conway, who was senior tutor of the House and about to go on sabbatical, that I would be replacing him for a year, having spent the two previous years as a baby dean. He also learned that I would be living in the senior tutor's apartment directly below his own digs, with Nancy, then pregnant with our first child, Lisa, who spent much of her first months asleep in a carriage surrounded by the walls of the little courtyard that separated the senior tutor's lodgings from those of the master of the House. "You know, John," Nock said to Conway, as he mused on this new and unwelcome knowledge, "I've always thought Herod was a much-maligned man."

As a sophomore I'd taken Nock's introductory course on the history of religion, mostly because I wanted something easy to round out a five course schedule. It was easy but not without reward: Nock would invite other faculty, sometimes of great distinction, to lecture on their specialty while Nock himself, instead of sitting discreetly in the audience, would occupy a chair on the lecture platform and there, invariably and conspicuously, fall asleep. The tension was palpable as (for one) Sir Hamilton A. R. Gibb lectured on Islam and Nock nodded to and fro, seriously threatening to fall into the arms of the anxious audience. It never happened, and I wondered if he was really asleep or just pretending. Filling in for Conway six years later, I paid Nock a courtesy call in the apartment above my own, there to find him surrounded by mountains of papers and books covering every inch of shelf and floor space, including the otherwise unused and unusable fireplace; it was the sanctum of an alien world. Had I persevered, I might, like Uncle Fred in Africa, have learned some of its mysteries. But I missed the chance. Nock was in fact a kind man who once, when a young tutor was mugged on a Cambridge street, offered to make up his loss, explaining that fortune had been good to him. It was said he had invested in Coca-Cola.

If Nock came from the ragtag margins of English society, the master of Eliot House, at whose Christmas party Nock disported himself so whimsically, was American gentry, the son of a college president who left the field of education to become an editor of the *New York Times*. This was the classicist John Huston Finley, probably the best known of all Harvard's legends-in-the-making. In fact he already was one when I arrived. When the pallid Nathan Pusey became Harvard's president, many assumed Finley wanted the job. Once I had heard him say he had reached third base, tenure at Harvard and the mastership of Eliot House, "on a bunt" (that is, a book on Pindar). What would home plate be if not the presidency? When I reported seeing him walk into Eliot House one day in spring 1953, together with the head of Harvard's governing board, it briefly excited speculation that his nomination was imminent. But it was not. Finley was not born to Harvard's presidency but to the mastership of Eliot House that he held for many years and on which he put his own indelible stamp.

Eliot House was Finley's lordship and we, students and faculty, were his thanes. As freshmen, we had to be interviewed by one of the tutors to be admitted to residence. As seniors, we were interviewed by Finley himself before he would write the letter that would get us into law school or medical school or graduate school. The letter of recommendation, Finley said later with mixed pride and self-deprecation, he had turned into an art form, and I regret that when I was his senior tutor I never rifled the files, as I had for my college board scores, to find out what he said about me. When I came across one of his recommendations for someone else, well after I'd moved across the country and discovered the world beyond the eastern seaboard, its lush rhetoric seemed faintly repellent. Time has been unkind to Mr. Chips. Yet Finley probably helped more people get Rhodes Scholarships than anyone else has ever done. He could also be honest and insightful. "Bliss," he said in my last interview with him, "you're trying to be a scholar among gentlemen and a gentleman among scholars, and sometime you'll have to decide which." I didn't dare say :"But you never have." But he was right: when I was elected to Phi Beta Kappa in the autumn of my senior year, a fellow member of the Owl Club, having read the news in Harvard's daily, *The Crimson*, looked at me and said in astonishment, "YOU?" I rejoiced in the duplicity of my double life.

Finley's genius was that of late Victorian camp. One year three roommates lived together in Eliot House whose names were Stephen Joyce, Paul Matisse, and Sadruddin Aga Khan. It was Finley's dream team. In an interview for *Time*, he said, "where but at Harvard," really meaning where but in his unique Eliot House, "where but at Harvard could you find in one room the grandson of the greatest of modern writers, the grandson of the greatest of modern painters, and the great-great-great-ad-infinitum grandson of God?" On another occasion, when the Eliot House football team was playing arch-rival Lowell House, Finley (it is told) said to Eliot Perkins, master of Lowell House, "Well, Perk, our fair-haired Achaeans are doing rather well against your plucky Trojans." To which the earthier Perkins replied (it is also told), "Fuck you, John." Looking back, I think Finley knew better than many of us that we lived in a post-feudal, post-epic world. He kept the past alive in the only way he could, like his eighteenth-century predecessors, in the codes of mock epic. I believe now, as I didn't realize at the time, that he was another ironist, just not one who wore his irony on his sleeve. Only an ironist, schooled in dramatic self-deprecation, would have said he reached third base on a bunt. But he was also that rarity, an ironist who could reach beyond or through irony to a virtuoso-like yet real sinceri- ty. At graduation he would find something kind and complimentary to say about every member of the class, perhaps a hundred seniors, as we walked up one by one to receive our diplomas.

Another of Finley's thanes who shaped the brilliant little community was Walter Jackson Bate, prodigiously gifted as a critic and lecturer and the biographer of both Johnson and Keats. An awkward boy who came to Harvard as an undergraduate from Indiana, he won prize after prize as a graduate student and, later, prize after prize for his books. He had a tongue as sharp and witty as his mind, and he held the older generation of scholars that had inflicted on him the philological penance of old Norse in withering contempt. He was also supremely adept at punctur- ing inflated reputations. The English Department had a secretary named Miss Jones, thought by most to be indispensable; Bate came to lunch at Eliot House one day and slid into his chair, groaning over his current job of chairing the English Department (a job he performed with almost ruthless skill) and therefore having to deal every day with the indispensable Miss Jones. "Maybe," he drawled, "maybe someday we can afford an electric typewriter and she'll electrocute herself." Or, of the venerable and pious Miltonist Douglas Bush, he said at another lunch, "I like Douglas," drawing out the long i of "like" and pausing half a moment for effect, "but he always looks like he just came out of a chamber of horrors."

Bate himself looked as though he had just gotten out of bed or en- countered an unruly plate of pasta. Seeing him at a meal, you couldn't help thinking of the much-rumpled Samuel Johnson, on whom Bate lavished his love and skill in lectures that were impersonations, not just interpretations, of Johnson. For decades of undergraduates, Bate *was* Johnson. The Boswell crowd at Yale he regarded as stuffy and pedantic. Johnson, who began in obscurity and poverty and became the symbol of his age, was Bate's moral hero, and for a time he became mine, thus for all his intellectual strength the hero I would need somehow to get beyond–that is, to learn not always to see the world through Bate's Johnsonian eyes. The danger in the presence of Harvard's great teachers was that of being forever in thrall, never outliving the master's spell, as happened to more than a few. Coming west, where the voices of Cambridge were fainter, turned out to be the lucky thing to do.

And then there was Conway, the Canadian veteran who had lost his right arm in the Italian campaign and, that rare thing in Cambridge, a practicing Roman Catholic who as senior tutor balanced Finley's mercurial whimsy with genuine saintliness. That he could light his cigarettes and tie his ties with his left hand seemed to express a veritable rage for the normal. Not until Jill Ker Conway published *True North*, the second volume of her memoirs and the sequel to *The Road from Coorain*, her story of growing up on the Australian outback, did I learn that the man she married in 1962 suffered from acute depressions and, as he told me not long before he died, went on walks from Cambridge to Concord and back, a distance of twenty-five miles or more.

Perhaps it was the depression, the *tedium vitae*, that made him so open to others, so utterly attentive. As an undergraduate, I would stop by his apartment on the first floor of K-entry some evenings, the same apartment as would later become briefly mine, knock hesitantly, and when I found him at home, he was invariably welcoming. "Come *in*," he would say. At the time this seemed generous; now it seems astonishing as I contemplate my own sullen dislike of being bothered when a student phones at night, just another in a string of solicitations and interruptions to the evening quiet. Miraculously, Conway seemed to value the conversations, full of my intellectual searchings for direction and secular meaning. For all its dazzle, Harvard was inhibiting, a place where everybody pretended to assume that everybody knew everything, where books were never admitted to having been read for the first time, only to having been re-read: e.g., "I was re-reading Sartre the other day, and…" This sort of affectation was a survival mechanism. But Conway was without affectation. He made it possible to believe one might not be forever inhibited, might move on from apprenticeship to something nearer mastery. And in his rectitude, he too offered the model of a father to be not only admired but challenged. Going to California enabled me to become, to the best of my ability, a prodigal, and I lost touch with John for a long time, partly because he married and left Cambridge to go to Toronto with Jill but also because I had too much else to do in the scurry of midlife and because I wasn't sure I would any longer have his approval. I was wrong about that. When we got together again, he in his 70s and I in my 60s, it was as if we were back in Cambridge in 1953 when our lives were nearer their start.

Conway knew the way of the world. He told a story of himself, as a naive and very young undergraduate at the University of British Columbia, when he was on the home debating team against a touring group from Oxford. The Oxonians were utterly sophisticated; the home team, not. One of the Oxonians was adept in using his text and his spectacles as props, rustling and rumpling the manuscript, putting on and taking off his glasses, gesturing with them and otherwise dominating the debate. After it was all over and Oxford had won, John went over to the Oxford lectern, there to discover that his opponent's props were blank paper and glasses with no glass in them. Though John was never anything but almost poignantly sincere, it was not because he had illusions about human disguises and maskings.

Bate and Conway–and Finley, too–not only filled the gap left by my father's death but also made academic skill seem an acceptable substitute for going to war and doing heroic things, for being an athlete, for being socially adept, for being all that I couldn't quite manage to be. They helped me believe in a community of mind in which those otherwise maladept were at no natural disadvantage. Conway's wound marked him, the most normal of men though also a warrior, as like all the rest of us both frail and different.

Eliot House in the 1950s was a last flowering of the genteel tradition. And, as much as Antonine Rome or the gilded age, the tradition bore within the seeds of its decline. The Harvard Houses, a princely gift of Edward Harkness, whose vast philanthropy earned him a front-page obituary in the *New York Times*, were big and brick and pseudo-Georgian, not unlike Wendover, and even their architecture was beginning to seem not timeless, like that of the seventeenth-century buildings in the Yard, but a bit out of date. John Finley's self-conscious rhetoric called ironic attention to its own mellifluous excess. The times weren't changing yet, at least not much, but they were about to. A tiny presentiment of change was the ending of maid service except for a weekly sweeping up of cigarettes that had been tossed by the hundreds into the fireplace. I think that was in my sophomore year. But maid service was not the heart of the story.

Up the road from Eliot House, where some of us luxuriated in wealth and satisfaction, maids or no maids, was Claverly Hall, where Harvard's underclass, students who lived at home because they couldn't afford otherwise or as a condition of their admission, spent part of their days before going back to Roxbury or Dorchester or to some less affluent section of Cambridge. In ten years at Harvard, four as an undergraduate and six more as a graduate student and apprentice administrator, I never once set foot in Claverly, never once (so far as I know) talked to a commuting student except when, as a baby dean, I had to interview freshmen who failed to meet the standards, and some who had the most conspicuous yet most mysterious difficulties were the commuters: I remember one in particular, polite, soft-spoken, apparently intelligent, but with a record of nothing but D's and F's, a record he promised to improve after midterms in the fall, again after finals in January, and once more after midterms in the spring, but that changed not at all for the better at year's end when he was asked to leave Harvard, most likely for good. I never had the least idea what the trouble was.

Minorities were few and also an underclass. Until after the war, blacks could not live in the dormitories: President Lowell–anti-immigration, anti-Semitic, and anti-integration–had been opposed. Change came slowly. One year, perhaps my own freshman year, the four black students in the class found themselves all rooming together. By the summer of 1954 when my turn came to assign freshmen to rooms and roommates, segregation had ended though very cautiously. I inherited a practice of writing students in any proposed grouping of whites and blacks to inquire, as delicately as possible, whether racist incompatibilities would result. It was awkward at best, but at the age of twenty-three, it didn't occur to me to do otherwise. Probably, in the context of the times, not much else could have been done without risking something worse. Nor did it occur to anybody, least of all myself, that the whole Byzantine business of trying to assign students to compatible roommates within the limits of a steeply graduated price structure was a kind of lunatic roulette with results guaranteed to displease almost everybody, just as they would have displeased me in 1949 if my roommate had not been so often and so obligingly absent. Once in a while I meet members of the classes of 1958 and 1959. At least two of them are colleagues at Stanford. When I confess to someone that I was responsible for his freshman room assignment, I always worry that I'm confessing to having created a disaster.

Even in those days the genteel tradition had its outright enemies, and at this distance I can see in the most commanding of them a figure as important in his way as Finley, Bate, or Conway, though he was the bad father and I hated him furiously. This was Perry Gilbert Eddy Miller, Ahab in tweeds, dark, driven, drunken, on his way to an early death, but palpably present and powerful, the nemesis of everything genteel, champion of the robust new world against the gentilities of the old, always on his own errand into the wilderness, and certainly not one of the Eliot House crowd.

In fact I didn't run into Miller until graduate school. Majoring in English history and literature or what I'd now call British history and literature, having in mind that "English" literature includes literature in English by Scots, Irish, Welsh and others, I had no time for our transatlantic culture, its history or literature or art. I had disliked *Walden* when I read it in tenth grade and, in a final examination, had been faced with ridiculous questions asking who was this or that person in the narrative, questions that would have required knowing the book by heart to answer. By the time I went to Harvard I was something of a classicist, something more of an Anglophile, and blind to the American tradition that Miller, together with the altogether different and estimable F.O. Matthiessen—a tragic figure in his suicide and his homosexuality—and others at Princeton, Berkeley, and elsewhere had tried to bring into the mainstream. When requirements for the Ph.D. finally obliged me to take Miller's introductory survey of American literature, I did so grudgingly, not only because of its subject but because it meant reverting to a beginner's role that I liked to think I'd outgrown. Miller's Hemingway-esque posturing encouraged my fastidious distaste. He always looked as if he might rip off his shirt and display what you were made to assume would be an extremely hairy chest. And when he came to *Moby Dick* , he was all Ahab, going on about true leadership and implying he had been a war hero, though rumor had it he spent most of his wartime in Paris cafés. Worst of all, he gave me a B for a paper on Whitman, sending me into a fury, partly of self-doubt. For a graduate student, a B was even then the next thing to failure. If pressed, however, I would have conceded it wasn't a good paper: I had nothing interesting to say about Whitman and wrote about him only because another essay I'd written on him at St. Paul's had won a prize, not surprisingly since it was the only submission–an essay that was also short on substance and rehashed some biographer's absurd proposition that Whitman wasn't really homosexual but rather something else, I'm not sure exactly what but maybe, preposterously, "auto-erotic." Angry as I was both at Miller and myself, I didn't give up and eventually wrote a complicated, new-critical sort of paper about the triadic structure of Hawthorne's novels that pleased him more. And in the longer run, perhaps Miller prevailed in my heart over the tradition of gentility, even the gentility of those to whom I owed almost everything.

Of course it's odd to think of Jack Bate, the rumpled latter-day Johnson, as genteel, but set beside Miller's America, Bate's eighteenth-century England preserved decorums, moral and social, for which Miller's America, full of demons and dark spirits, had small respect. And when it came to writing a dissertation, eighteenth-century Britain, I had no doubt, was the place for me. Even then, the impulses of obedience and resistance were contending, though sublimated into academic expression. Swift, on whom I'd written a senior essay as an undergraduate, is the most subversive of satirists, but my subject had been his sermons, the most dutiful of his utterance, which he himself dismissed as second-rate. Having now to produce a dissertation, I turned again to a satirist and a radical one at that, but in the far from radical spirit of finding a subject that hadn't been adequately "done," thus ending up with the minor mid-century poet Charles Churchill who, having died young, left behind him a manageable output of verse that fit into a single volume. In fact not a whole lot needed to be "done" about Churchill, and the dissertation had the despairing aspect of projects undertaken in the hope of going where few have gone before but where almost no one has any serious desire to go.

I like the story of another Harvard Ph.D. who, having become a serious scholar, took measures to ensure that the embarrassment of his dissertation would not survive him. The story is, he and a co-conspirator more or less simultaneously called up from the archives the two existing copies of the dissertation. After suitable time had passed the co-conspirator departed, leaving his copy on the trolley that would convey it back to the archives. Then, while no one was looking, the author too slipped out, scooping up the copy from the trolley and secreting it, together with the other and only remaining one, so as to remove both from the archives forever and consign them to the trash bin or the flames. I admire this derring-do but not having had the nerve to replicate it, take comfort in the hope that in almost four decades probably no one has ever called up "Charles Churchill: A Critical Study" from its quiet resting place. But since Harvard, needing more shelf space, recently rid itself of second copies of dissertations, the logistics of a theft have grown less formidable. The temptation doesn't go away.

However undistinguished the dissertation, getting a job was not hard. I didn't get the one at Princeton that I spent a day of interviews and lunch at the Nassau Inn in pursuit of, but had I been offered and taken it, it would have been a mistake; Princeton was too near Wendover as well as too near Cambridge and also too hierarchic–mailboxes in the history department were said to be arranged not alphabetically but in order of seniority–to have effaced the desire to combine scholarship and gentility. I also didn't get a job at Dartmouth that took a day of interviews in the gloom of late autumn in Hanover. Over the years I've interviewed for quite a few positions–directorships of libraries, for example–that I didn't get: I think I do badly in the presence of unfamiliar authority. But I had taken a seminar in summer, 1958, with the head of Stanford's English Department, then visiting Harvard, a Renaissance scholar of much-repressed sexuality who ruled his domain so autocratically that when I wrote inquiring about a position, he replied by return mail offering me an instructorship at $5,700 a year; no interview required, no visit, no presentation of a paper, none of the hoops that candidates have to leap through now, not to mention none of the pain. So on a bright June morning in 1960, I headed west from Wendover in an aging Ford station wagon, never before having been past Pittsburgh. Nancy, pregnant with Peter, and our first two children, Lisa (then three) and Sarah (not yet one), were to follow by train since I couldn't bear to think of them on an airplane. The car's front exhaust pipe gave out in Madison, Wisconsin, where I had stopped to visit a friend, and the transmission housing gave out after hours of threatening noises as I crossed a bridge over the Missouri in Chamberlain, South Dakota. But I was not long delayed in either place. Miraculously a service station in Chamberlain had in stock a replacement for the housing.

After another day or two of travel, having passed through the Black Hills, I came over a little rise in the road in the plains of eastern

Wyoming and saw, with a gasp, the Big Horn mountains. I spent the night in Buffalo, where the bar was full of cowboys on evening furlough from the neighboring ranches. A day or so later I crossed the Salt Lake desert at four in the morning, fearing that the car might not survive the heat of the day and, like other travelers on the roads, carrying a water bag on the front, though I wasn't sure whether it was for emergency use in the radiator or emergency use for me, should I get stranded out there in the glare of the sun on white sands. At the Utah-Nevada border I came through a desolate little gambling town named Wendover and wondered what its inhabitants would think if they were to see that other Wendover across the continent. I went through Donner Pass on July 4th and on down to the valley floor where the temperature was over 100 degrees. I annoyed a gas station attendant in Sacramento: "Is it always this hot here?" He looked sullen and barely answered. Nearing San Francisco, I twirled the dial and found the Giants. I drove down the east side of San Francisco Bay and crossed one of the bridges, not having understood from the map that I should have taken the Bay Bridge through the city. Seeing my Massachusetts plates, the toll taker asked where I was going. I said Palo Alto and he said, "Lots of rich people live there." I drove up the main avenue into Stanford, lined with tall palms. I gasped again–"Jesus!" I think I said–this time at the landscape and the Spanish architecture. It was all sandstone and tile, palms and live oaks, alien to the eye. The brick and ivy of Harvard and Eliot House, the elms and maples and tulip trees of Wendover, were far away.

"How Do You Like California?"

Stanford is big, brassy, rich (if not so rich as Harvard or, *per capita*, as St. Paul's or the Milton Hershey school for the needy), not certain of its place in the intellectual world, full of more first-class athletes than any other American university, just over a hundred years old, a meat-and-potatoes institution in which subjects like Islamic architecture and Sumerian or Celtic studies that embellish the curricula of a few universities like Harvard and Chicago have no place but in which engineering is for many a way of life. The university still bears the stamp of Leland

Stanford, the railroad baron and governor of the state whose portraits radiate a somber ferocity and whose university is not the less a lovingly sentimental memorial to his son Leland, Jr., dead in Florence at sixteen. Leland and his wife, Jane, wanted their university to be a practical place, devoted to the knowledge of everyday, where talented youth from the American West could acquire knowledge both morally and intellectually useful. Being conservative, though not more so than most universities, Stanford preserves the character that Leland and Jane, who kept it going in the hard times after her husband's death, had in mind (leaving aside that in the beginning it was tuition-free but now costs many thousands): it is still eminently practical, sentimental rather than self-satisfied in some of its self-representations, and compared to its Ivy League rivals on the other coast, raw and new.

Stanford is Californian through and through, never ceasing to hope that the time will come when it outdraws Harvard in the annual competition, a competition only thinkable since Stanford's postwar rise, to see which of the two universities will draw the larger number of students admitted to both, a competition that so far Harvard has won every time and most likely will keep on winning. Yet Stanford is so different from Harvard demographically and intellectually that any standard of comparison is grossly imprecise. Perhaps 1,000 of Stanford's undergraduates major in engineering while Harvard's population of engineers is minute. If Stanford wants to compete, it could almost as well compete with M.I.T. except that M.I.T. has few students in the liberal arts. Stanford's humanists sometimes bridle at the power and prevalence of engineering and cranky letters from retired humanists to the local press lament the end of culture, an event for which engineeering and computer science are held responsible, but I've no doubt that an entente between the humanities and engineering is the best thing to hope for. Despite well-intended efforts, including some of my own, the reconciliation has never quite come about. If it did, maybe Stanford could worry less about whether it bests Harvard, or *vice-versa*, in the annual admissions war. Perhaps it might even win the war sometime.

When I arrived in 1960, the English Department, like the university as a whole, was expanding fast, with new Ph.D.'s arriving from all over–Berkeley, Columbia, Oxford, Harvard, even a couple from Stanford, notwithstanding the department's rule against hiring its own graduate students. We all got along, sharing the usual beginners' impatience with our elders. Because the department had a practice, different from Harvard's or Yale's, of not hiring anyone unless a tenure position was in sight after six years' probation, we were not in the muted competition with each other that scars the human environment at Cambridge and New Haven. Nor, contrary to those who believe nature should be as red as possible in tooth and claw, do I think the department was greatly the worse for its benign environment. Even so, being at a university, any university under any circumstances with any set of colleagues, is a tangled mix of collegiality and competition for whatever reputation, modest or no, the academy can offer. John Updike, who graduated from Harvard the year after I did, refers to "the modest sort" of celebrity "that comes to writers," and perhaps it is a Harvard-related tic to think of one's own celebrity as "modest," whether it is the truly modest celebrity to be had in the academy or the not-quite-so-modest celebrity of writers like Updike. But the academic itch for even modest local fame is chronic, and the university is more like a tower of glass and fragile egos than anything so solid as ivory.

Looking back on the humiliations of the golf course and the ski slope yields a perverse ecstasy; looking back on life in the university yields a kind of lingering middle-of-the-night insomniac trepidation, the anxiety of one in the morning to three, or two in the morning to four–whether more or less acute, there's no way to know, than if I'd not exchanged Ivy League ivy for Spanish tile and the edgy self-satisfactions of Harvard, sure of its own preeminence, for the laid-back insecurities of Stanford, always needing to tell the world and to be told that it is a "world-class" university.

The first question everyone asked when I arrived was "How do you like California?" and the right answer, it was easy to tell, was "a lot." That was not a lie, but it was a partial truth I didn't want to be pressured into. For one thing, I'd made up my mind I wasn't going to fall for San Francisco the way everybody else did, and what's more, the Giants were inconveniently located there. That resolve lasted only until I saw the city's hills and fog and water and bridges. But if I was going to like California and Stanford and San Francisco, it would have to be on my terms. At Harvard who would say to a newcomer "How do you like Boston?" Boston isn't there to be liked; it's just there. Hence the Boston dowager stories. For example, Boston dowager greets Harvard freshman, "Where do you come from?" Freshman says, "Iowa, ma'am." Boston dowager says, "Oh, in Boston we call it Ohio." Or, Boston dowager says to a freshman just arrived from California, "How did you get here?" Freshman says he took the train for three days. Dowager replies, "That's nice, I'd like to do that," then pauses:"But of course I'm already here."

Even harder to imagine than "How do you like Boston" is "How do you like Massachusetts?" Massachusetts is not a metaphor like California, and Bostonians think of the western part of their state–especially Springfield, where my first wife came from and where most Bostonians have never been, therefore missing Erastus Salisbury Field's grand "Historical Monument of the American Republic" in the Springfield Museum, a painting that will make an appearance in the next chapter– as *terra incognita*, like everything beyond the Hudson River in Steinberg's rendering of the Manhattanite's map, a place more remote even than San Francisco. As for Stanford, I did come to like it and to think it was about as good a place as I could have found to spend almost forty years. I also came to like it because it was a place where, more than once, I fell in love. In universities public work and private life have a way of becoming deeply intertwined.

When I arrived, my teaching experience had consisted solely of tutorial sessions, one on one. I had never taught freshman English, never given a lecture. I was scared and spent the entire summer of 1960 writing out by hand on lined paper forty lectures, mostly dull, for English 7, "Masterpieces of English Literature," an old standard routinely assigned to newcomers. During one lecture a steam pipe in the antiquated classroom, only a few feet in front of the lectern, had begun an uneven dripping, but I was fixed on the middle distance and couldn't tell for several minutes what was happening. I only knew there was a disturbance in my visual field; I thought perhaps someone was throwing something at me. Ever since, my anxiety dreams about teaching (almost every teacher has them, counterparts to the unprepared-for-the-exam dream that disturbs the sleep of former undergraduates) have played variations on the theme of classroom insurrection. I also had to teach two sections of freshman English, twenty students in each, who wrote a paper each week. When autumn was over, I had graded 400 papers, fifty hour exams, and fifty final exams. I went to a shoe repair shop and sat doing nothing for an hour, waiting for my shoes to be resoled.

Though there was less teaching to be done as the years went on, teaching itself never got much easier, especially not after "teaching evaluations" were created in the 1970s. Other than universities, where do sixty-year-olds ask twenty-year-olds to grade their performance as excellent, good, fair, or poor, not identifying themselves except by how often they went to class and barely realizing that the dean will see the results? At the end of term, you hand out evaluation forms, ask one of the students to collect and deliver them to the registrar, then absent yourself from the room and wait six weeks for the results. Once a benign undergraduate said, "I don't like to criticize professors, especially when they are as nice as Carnochan, but he really isn't very good." Verdict:"fair," no doubt because the respondent was feeling too kind to check "poor." Of course there have been "goods" and "excellents," too –even, on two cherished occasions, nothing but "excellents"; both classes were small–and a few students to whom I hope I've passed on something of the passion that Bate passed on to me. But it's the "fairs" and the "poors" that you remember with raw feelings, whether in evaluations by students or readings of your manuscript or reviews of what you've published. With no trouble at all, I remember that Martin Price didn't like my book on Swift in the 60s, Howard Weinbrot didn't like a piece on satire that I published in *PMLA* (the profession's house organ) in the 70s, Patricia Craddock didn't like my book on Gibbon in the 80s (and neither did the reader–I think I know who it was–who first reported on it as a manuscript), Alvin Kernan didn't like my book on the American curriculum in the 90s, and Claude Rawson didn't like my review of a book of his in 1995, accusing me of the reviewer's worst sin, that of not having bothered to read the book (but I did read it, every last impacted word). All these names carry some weight in the academy. Yet I also remember, with surpassing gratitude, Pat Rogers's review of *Confinement and Flight*, my midlife crisis book of the mid-1970s sheltering private crisis under the mantle of the scholarly. I should have taken Rogers's generosity as a model more often than I've done.

Not only does getting evaluations and reviews generate anxiety, so does giving them, especially grades, which translate readily into future lives and careers. Complaints about grade inflation are blind to actual facts, namely, that even though grades have gone up, and even if absolutely no one were to get any grade less than a B- (some do but, it's true, not many), what's left is a fiercely compressed six point scale–A+ (rarely), A, A-, B+, B, B--that locates individual performances with not wholly arbitrary precision. Any kind of A is good, and an A+ signals something extraordinary. Any kind of B is definitely not so good, and the plusses and minuses count a lot. A- means: good but I (the giver of the grade) had to think about it. B+ means: nice try but you're not quite over the threshold. B means: this is OK. B- means: this is barely OK and probably I should have given it a C+, if I were being honest. Any kind of C is bad. Everybody in the universities understands this scale, knows how to read it (imagine how a transcript of B's and B-'s looks beside one with all A's), and the need to decide whether this paper or that exam gets an A- or a B+ is a nagging sore. In the case of graduate students, the decisions are even more a burden. When he gave me the B, Perry Miller was saying: you really don't belong in this business. I doubt that he felt any compunction in delivering his verdict, but is it foolish or cowardly to fret over decisions so laden with human consequences?

Compared to the anxieties of teaching, those of administration are in some ways less trying. In cloistered offices and conference rooms where administrators spend much of their time, the outside world is excluded. So the fifteen years, more or less, that I spent doing administrative chores were probably motivated as much by wanting to spend less time in the classroom as by that old, fleeting thought in 1953 that in twenty-five years I might be walking through Harvard Yard with the casual stride of a president-elect. While I was senior tutor of Eliot House, Perry Miller said to me once that university administration should be left to janitors. I resented the sneer on behalf of the janitors as much as for myself but acknowledge that being an administrator often means emptying bureaucratic wastepaper baskets and tidying up debris. On one occasion when Stanford was cutting its budget, I heard Wolfgang Panofsky, then the director of the Stanford Linear Accelerator, explain that what he did was slash janitorial service until people complained their wastebaskets were overflowing, then restore it enough to make them feel better. I thought that got to the heart of the matter.

If you want to do administration, you often have to claim that administration is the last thing you want to do. There are usually grains of truth, sometimes more than a few, in the pose of reluctance. If the tedium of the administrative conference room affords restful moments, there are less sleepy times. As dean of graduate studies, I had occasional run-ins with the feudal barons who run departments in the medical school, always feeling like the country mouse visiting the big city. Yet going to the city is heady business. After the trip is over, you think, well, that was good, I was lucky, I survived.

Even two years of chairing the English Department, a less difficult assignment then than now when more prickly personalities prowl the department halls (including myself: age prickles), left me with the feeling of having survived. I also learned that congenital double vision isn't always a bad thing, practically speaking. In the winter and spring of 1971, Bruce Franklin, now the holder of a chair at Rutgers University in Newark, then a tenured associate professor in the Stanford English department, disrupted the campus with speeches and calls to action in response to events in Southeast Asia. Franklin maintained everything he said was protected by the First Amendment, a defensible proposition because he chose his wild words with utmost care. The administration couldn't afford to worry much about free speech and, seeing the campus coming to pieces, suspended Franklin and scheduled a hearing, lawyers and all, before the president's advisory board. The board, made up of faculty elected from different constituencies, is at the top of Stanford's chain of committees. In the fall it would hear the case and recommend whether Franklin should be fired. Stakes were high.

Meanwhile, the English Department needed a new chair to replace Ian Watt, famous (or "modestly" so) as author of *The Rise of the Novel*, a work that turned postwar literary study away from poetry and towards fiction and the sociology of culture. During the war, Watt had been a prisoner in the camp on the River Kwai and, chairing the department in a time of troubles, he displayed an agility of mind that suggested how he endured conditions on the Kwai. Now that his term was over, with the Franklin hearings scheduled for the fall and the department deeply divided, finding someone willing to follow him was not easy. But I confess to having covertly desired the undesirable.

The process, like so many in the academy, was cumbersome. First the department took a confidential but not a binding vote. Then the results were passed on to the dean's office. Then the dean interviewed the department faculty. The results of the vote, as best I can guess, were inconclusive, and Gordon Wright, a French historian whose distinction as a scholar was exceeded only by his decency as a person, had to sort it all out. When he turned to me, having no doubt exhausted the supply of candidates higher on the list, it must have been in some desperation. Not only had I been an associate professor for just three years, hence short on seniority, I was also Bruce's friend and up to a point his ally: whatever commotion he had caused, I too believed he hadn't over-stepped the line between protected speech and crying "fire" in a crowd-ed theater and believed it more confidently when I heard Alan Der-showitz, not so well known then as now after the von Bülow and Simpson cases, argue the question with Stanford's Gerald Gunther be-fore an ACLU meeting in San Francisco. So I was not in favor with those beyond the dean's office who would have to approve the appoint-ment. But driven by a mix of ambition, obligation, and the desire to show I could do it, I said I'd take the job for a year. Gordon Wright, whatever his inner inquietude, was steadfast. If the appointment wasn't approved, he said (I learned much later) that he would resign. Finally it was approved after the scuffling that led Wright to take a stand, and I did the job not for one but two years.

Though they were not easy years, they were not so hard as they might have been, for the assignment suited someone habitually of two minds. With the department divided 50-50 for Franklin and against, it was easy to resist calls from his defenders, mostly younger faculty, for a depart-mental statement: none could ever be approved, no matter what it might have said. Waiting and keeping up everyday business were the only things to do. And as I watched the hearings day after day, from about halfway up in the Physics Tank, an ugly circular building (by now mercifully demolished) with an auditorium of sharply raked seats, I felt detached, suspended above the proceedings like some aerial balloonist or like the eighteenth- and nineteenth-century poets who wrote verse about what they saw from a hilltop looking down, or like my young self scanning the Wendover landscape or watching the life of Harvard Square from the fourth floor of Straus Hall. I still think Franklin, how-ever disruptive, was within his civil rights, but it's not hard to see why the administration said he wasn't. The advisory board voted five to two to fire him, the two dissenters, Stanford's future president Don Kennedy and the theologian Robert McAfee Brown, voting instead for suspension. The president and trustees did what they had asked the board to ask them to do. Years of litigation followed, the ACLU and Franklin challenging the university but eventually losing in the courts.

Two years later I became a dean myself, but the deanship was that of graduate studies, an odd hybrid lacking line authority and afflicted by a cloudy sense of purpose. A group of graduate deans from five Ivy

League and two West Coast universities met twice a year and, even after its numbers were augmented, continued to call itself (with no premonition of being politically incorrect; perhaps the name has been changed by now) the Seven Dwarves. Hotel bulletin boards would announce that the Dwarves were meeting in the Cavalier Room or the Michelangelo Suite, no doubt to the surprise of happenstance observers. When I left the deanery in 1980, the provost abolished the position. Since then it has had several reincarnations, but its moneys have been reallocated. After I resigned and the position had been eliminated, I received some notes regretting the provost's insensitivity. But I didn't much mind having helped to make the job redundant.

In it I had learned some elementary truths: that universities are big and complicated; that therefore change can't help being slow; that waiting (again) isn't always a bad idea. I also learned that losing a vote in the academic senate as I did, especially if it is early in your tenure, can be less hurtful than watching your team lose a World Series. And I learned for good and all what I had begun to know as a baby dean at Harvard, when I gave advice to befuddled ex-valedictorians and once had to cope with a threatened suicide, or as chair of the Stanford English Department when I once had to cope with a homicidal graduate student and fought with the deans over tenure disputes: that administration not only is emptying wastebaskets and watching opposing armies clash but is also an arena of others' pain.

The Business School produced the largest number of the damaged. Each year one or two students who failed accounting or finance were dismissed and, dreams of prosperity shattered, would file a grievance, not unreasonably because Business School policies on academic performance combined stringency and ambiguity. The code had been devised by someone or some committee intent on being tough and business-like but deficient in powers of expression and coherence. Eventually repairs were made but not before considerable damage had been done. Not that the Business School was the only source of trouble. Students ran afoul of their dissertation advisors. Faculty who were denied tenure filed grievances, generally alleging–in the case of minorities and women–discrimination. My charge included hearing these complaints, and I cringed inwardly as I clambered up the stairs at eight o'clock every morning to encounter the sad stories.

Yet the five years (I had promised myself I would get out before I was fifty) weren't a waste of time, and not just because I left office with no more fear of flying. The truths I had absorbed, elementary though they were, would never have come home to me in the walled garden of the English Department. And the tardy insight that universities are big, complicated places where things get done slowly pointed the way to a task I would not have ventured before. Of eighteenth-century British writers, the one I should have tackled seriously but hadn't was Gibbon. So I decided to read the *Decline and Fall of the Roman Empire*, all 3,500 pages of it and all fifteen centuries from Rome of the Antonines to the fall of Byzantium in 1453. But if I were to spend months reading the *Decline and Fall*, there had to be a payoff, namely another book. I got a fellowship to write one, though I had only a vague idea of what it might turn out to be about. I was lucky to get the fellowship: I have never mastered the art of grantsmanship, which consists of proposing a project as conceptually finished and needing only to be translated into print, even though most grant-seekers are as uncertain as I was about what the project may eventually look like.

Turning to Gibbon meant writing about someone whom Samuel Johnson, a father figure's father figure of college days, had regarded with muscular contempt, though Jack Bate himself did not. In the long run, that daily slow march up the stairs of the deanery led me to find value in the enormous work and constricted life of the flabby little historian whose finicky ways and heretical skepticism subjected him to Johnsonian scorn and made him, except in his ironic powers, quite unlike the Swift I so admired. I called the book *Gibbon's Solitude: The Inward World of the Historian*. For he was very much a solitary, the only survivor among seven siblings, nurtured by an aunt after his mother died in childbirth, living his life more in the library than in the world, never marrying despite an early unconsummated affair of the heart with a young Swiss woman who later became the wife of Jacques Necker, France's powerful minister of finance in the ancien régime, making friends with difficulty but inspiring deep loyalty in a few. Unprepossessing as he was, even comical, I came to see him as a courageous and good man. His anxieties more than matched mine–he never got up the nerve to make a maiden speech in Parliament, though he tried–which contributed to my admiration. Courage comes in more than one guise.

Not only did Gibbon devote himself with daily resolve, and for years, to writing the *Decline and Fall*, he was also able to see himself, the magisterial historian, with insouciance. In his thirties he developed a swelling in his groin; whether it was a hernia or a hydrocele is still a question. The physician he consulted said, "Come back in a week," which he didn't do. The swelling then stayed with him all his life, eventually growing to such humiliating size that he had to stop pretending it didn't exist and consult another physician, to whom he posed a riddle: "Why is a fat man"–by this time Gibbon was very fat–"like a Cornishman"? The answer:"Because neither one ever sees his member." Gibbon had represented a Cornish borough in Parliament, and the pun was double-edged. In his rather short life–he died at fifty-seven, probably of septicemia after a third operation for the great swelling–Gibbon worked hard and didn't complain. He was not a grievant.

After Gibbon there came a job that I unambiguously wanted, so much so that I violated the protocols of reluctance and told the search committee I would like it. The six years I then spent as director of the Stanford Humanities Center were the best of my life at the university. Not that the job was anxiety-free, for it required the care and feeding of important and self-important visitors and also the organizing of conferences, an occupation like that of a theatrical producer or a boxing promoter, often spent in nervously counting the house. But the anxiety was infrequent, the staff was unsurpassably good, and fellows of the Center, unlike petitioners at the graduate dean's office, had reason to be cheerful, as they almost always were: twenty to thirty people a year–graduate students, Stanford faculty, faculty from elsewhere, including universities in Peru and Mexico and Ghana, historians, philosophers, political scientists, literary scholars who all shared for a year a common enthusiasm for learning and sometimes a kind of giddy elation. In spring 1986, we commemorated the 650th anniversary of Petrarch's celebrated ascent of Mount Ventoux, said to be the first time anybody climbed a mountain just because it was there. Ours was nothing more than a hike up a local hill to yet another panoramic view, this one of the San Francisco Bay and peninsula, but we all wore pale blue T-shirts with an image of Petrarch's mountain and the dates "1336-1986."

Being at the Center meant learning better to understand disciplines besides English. Unlike scientists whose language is trans-national, even unlike students of comparative literature, students and teachers of English labor under the burden of the parochial. Often we speak no other language well, and for all its power, literature in English is only a sliver of the literature of the world. If being a dean freed me from the Johnsonian spell, being director of the Center freed me from "English" and the boundaries of the eighteenth century. Before, I had only been able to imagine myself as a specialist in a field or (striving for greater cachet) a "dix-huitièmiste." Now I wanted to say something about American higher education. That meant another book.

While I was at the Center, the demagogues of the right, Bloom and Bennett and Cheney and D'Souza, had fought with the universities, Stanford especially, in a debate that left the public limp and baffled in the face of questions like the necessity (or not) of reading Dante, doubtless an important matter but not life-and-death as Bloom and the rest made it seem. I confess I didn't read Dante, and even then not all of him, until I was fifty and had to teach the *Inferno* in a freshman class. I should have read him earlier, but I should have read other things, too, like Hegel's *Phenomenology*, that I didn't and still haven't and no doubt never will. Not reading everything (can anybody, really?) or not reading any particular text has nothing essential to do with being a citizen, contrary to self-serving claims that not reading Dante or Hegel impairs the civic and moral faculties. The battles of the late 1980s were about political advantage. With the realities of American higher education and its actual mechanisms of change, they had little to do. I wanted to look at some of the realities.

The curriculum wars of the eighties, far from being new and strange, had (I said) been going on in one skirmish after another ever since Charles Eliot became president of Harvard in 1869 and, over forty years, dismantled the classical curriculum and its requirements, replacing it with a "free elective" system that allowed students to graduate with sixteen credits in almost any courses they chose. I also said that the combatants of the eighties, whether in politics or in the academy, either knew nothing about the history of American higher education or ignored it as an inconvenience to their argument. This is indisputable. It is a puzzle that universities, charged with helping to preserve the past, know so little of their own. Not that knowing the history of higher education will eliminate conflict any more than knowledge of old wars will avert new ones. But if nothing is to be gained by knowing something about how we got to where we are, if history is all bunk, half the subjects of university study might as well be given up. Even so my claim that the curriculum wars were just aftershocks of Eliot's earthquake was not congenial to the reviewer in the very conservative *Washington Times* ("Mr. Carnochan evidently has standards for liberal education, but they are low") or to Alvin Kernan (who was Princeton's graduate dean at the same time as I was Stanford's) or to anyone who believed that a revolution was taking place in American higher education and that universities were headed for the abyss. I think this was nonsense and believe that Larry Levine in his book called, *contra* Bloom, *The Opening of the American Mind*, got it right: the genius of American education has been its adaptive habit, however gradual–its dynamic, however deliberate, of social change. If anything has been amiss in American education, it is not instability but too rabid a desire to impose stability: why should Stanford, with its 1,000 engineers, serve up the same educational menu as Harvard, whose most famous engineer, later to found Microsoft, packed his bags after a year or two and made many billions without benefit, most likely, of being able to recite the seven deadly sins? Liberal education is not a single thing. If it were, it would not be liberal at all.

Some look for continuity in history and find it. Others look for rupture and also find it. Though I lean to the former camp, no one could deny that something is always the same, something always different. Politicians and social critics lean to the second camp because angry cries of "revolution!" get more attention than claims that not much is new; historians, being historians, more often belong to the first. Even in the case of real revolutions like those of France, Russia, and America or the educational revolution of Charles Eliot, when something has really changed and it's impossible to shrug and say, "plus ça change," some will want to know the cause–that is, the antecedents of change– while others will want more to understand what happened day-by-day. The educational "revolution" of the 1980s, like the Republican "revolution" of 1994, was really no revolution at all except in the minds of partisans on both sides.

I hoped, fondly, that this book would make me more modestly famous. One friend joked, while I was writing it, that she expected to see me with Barbara Walters. Allan Bloom, after all, had sold many thousands of copies. But I didn't, and who now remembers Allan Bloom anyhow? An article about the book appeared in the *New York Times* but never a review. I spent an hour or more with a *Times* photographer–the brilliant Chester Higgins, whose work on African and African-American themes is memorably fine–but no picture ever appeared, though I suppose one or another of Higgins's images may have found its way to the paper's morgue. A feature and a photograph appeared in the *Chronicle of Higher Education*. I was interviewed by a National Public Radio station, not in New York or San Francisco but in Albany. Perhaps all that constitutes a tiny increment of modest fame.

If the educational revolution of the 1980s was a political chimera, there was one real revolution in the past forty years that has changed higher education massively, and that was the event called "the sixties," even though a good part of it took place in the seventies. The changes the sixties brought to the curriculum were not the main thing: less consequential than they seemed then, they were a partial reversion to Eliot's free elective system and were short-lived. What really changed, radically and permanently, was the social fabric of the university, as public work and private lives came tumultuously closer together amidst riots, burnings, broken windows, and sometimes even death. For those charged with the public order, it was a terrible time. But for those brought up on the habits of the 1940s and 1950s who then found their way into the academy, a main site, as much as Woodstock or Haight-Ashbury, of "the sixties," the time was ablaze with excitement and life and (what else?) sex. John Updike says he is surprised "to find, in fiction written by women of roughly my generation, the period of protests and marches recalled as a wonderful time." It surprises me that Updike is surprised. It also surprises me, if it's true, that only women write fondly of those days. Surely there have been some men before now who have confessed to enjoying it all?

In the sixties, the students were not much younger than ourselves, and they seemed to be enjoying themselves hugely. Not for them was reading every assignment twice, or even once. There were other things to do, and in a cause that most of them and many of us believed in genuinely: the folly of the Vietnam War. At one moment of crisis, with a political rally about to begin, a group of four or five undergraduates came around the corner of Stanford's memorial church chanting mellifluously, "Up against the wall, motherfuckers." By now they're probably middle-aged lawyers, and they didn't have or even really want an army to carry their orders, but they were having a good time. Only ten years before, I'd been pecking away dutifully in my never-to-be-improved upon, one-fingered fashion at "Charles Churchill: A Critical

Study." I wondered if students in Harvard Yard were by now also chanting "Up against the wall…" The Victorian world had crumbled, its authority gone. It was a mercy that Sibyll died in 1966. Had she lived, she would have been stricken. And, having been at pains to warn me, at whatever cost to her modesty, about the dangers of unwanted pregnancies and getting married too early, all this in connection with the febrile affair with Cassie that she surely guessed at, she would have been scandalized if she were to have caught a hint of what I was up to, even before her death, in faraway California. Her death made some things easier for me, as deaths of parents will often do.

Teaching is an erotic activity, and so is learning, and no threats or legislation regarding sexual harassment are going to affect that fact one whit. Jonathan Swift became Esther Johnson's tutor when she was six and never fell out of love with her. Small wonder that in the heady atmosphere of the sixties, with their summers of love and triumphs of birth control, passions flared and filled the air with adventure. Finally it was time to make up for the uncomfortable contortions of the back seat (had it only been the Rolls-Royce instead of a 1950 Plymouth, into which a policeman once shone his embarrassing light, it would have been a more comfortable back seat) and for anguished fears of pregnancy: Cassie's mixed-up menstrual cycle regularly filled me with panic that on one occasion almost but not quite disrupted my compulsive preparation for final exams.

Robert Nozick, who was Peter's senior thesis adviser and with whom he and I once shared an ice cream cone in Harvard Square, compares falling in love with holding hands and walking into the water together, step by step. It is a lovely analogy: the first steps are careful, for the waters are cold and unfamiliar to the body, no matter how often you have stepped into the same ocean before. Then you go faster and more confidently. And finally take the plunge. I don't think I ever sexually harassed anybody (though I recall two undergraduates who did in their minor way harass me), if only because I was shy and fearful of rejection. So the wonder always is, how to get to the place where we want to be? How can we tell (Nozick again) that each will "recognize" the other since "neither wants to recognize if the other does not?" How could I ever overcome the fearfulness of not being recognized? The sixties helped fearful people dare to try the water. Three times it happened, as Thomas Wyatt put it in a sonnet, "in special" (which to scan right has to be pronounced "in spe-ci-al").

The feelings come back in dream images, like spots of Wordsworthi-an time. The first: I've been in the East visiting my mother who is dying and I'm waiting fearfully to catch a plane home. Then somehow a telegram reaches me, or is it a note, with three words of a new Beatles song, "in my life," but I don't know, though I do, what the words mean because I haven't heard the song.

The second: on route 280, "the world's most beautiful freeway," two of us on the way to San Francisco on an August day in the early seven-ties as a cold summer fog swirls and obscures the panorama of the Bay. It is the start of a new life that lasts only a few months and ends sadly, after I've drawn back, in a ride to the airport just before Christmas. I want to go to the gate, knowing that it's an ending. She says no, also knowing that it's an ending, "No, it's too much, too much."

But then, third time lucky, a few years later: I'm off duty one day from my public life as a dean, and a bed collapses *in medias res*. We laugh helplessly, the start of twenty animating years, dream turning now into waking. Life in the dean's office had its bright, if invisible, side.

So that is why I like California, should anybody happen now to ask. If not for Leland and Jane's memorial to their lost son, none of this would have happened as it did, with whom it did. The journey across plains, mountains, and deserts was a luckier trek than I could have expected when I headed west from Wendover. Why snivel about the anxieties of being a teacher or being a dean when other some waters have been so exhilarating?

The "Girl in Red"

David Smith, the American metalworker-turned-sculptor who helped bring on the sea change that refashioned American art and all the art of the West after the second war, said: "Provincialism or coarseness or un-culture is greater for creating art than finesse or polish. Creative art has a better chance of developing from coarseness and courage than from culture. One of the good things about American art is that it doesn't have the spit and polish that some foreign art has. It is sparse." When

I read this in 1969, I found myself nodding an assent. Looking at it now, I realize that the words, or the thought, could have come from the demoniac Perry Miller, the old enemy.

Had Miller touched me in some unfamiliar recess of the mind? Not long after the indignity of the B he gave me, I opened the Boston Sunday paper one morning at breakfast, there to find an image of Erastus Salisbury Field's portrait of the Moore family from Ware, Massachusetts (ca. 1839), a massive grouping of father, mother, and four children, marked by the combination of sparseness and ornament, of the somber and the colorful, that gives much American art its particular feel, folk art and high modern art alike. Think of Sam Francis's big canvases, whiter than white (like Melville's whale), as sparse as can be at the center but with a strip of rainbow color at the margins, never enclosing the whiteness but tempering it with a riot of what seems like refracted light. The sparseness that David Smith values is not the whole story, for it is often only the ground on which figures of ornament or power are drawn, just as, in "Joseph Moore and His Family," the dark clothes of the husband, wife and three boys set off the little girl's white dress and the riotously rich pattern of the carpet that lights up the foreground.

Seeing "Joseph Moore and His Family" started me down the road of desire that later yielded the mixed blessing of a collection, a desire no doubt enhanced by atavistic memories of Blisses and Baldwins, of Farnhams and Lambards, New England ancestors all, products of the same rocky soil on which were grafted the rich textures of the old world. When asked how I got started collecting, I say that when I saw the Moore family, I thought: if I ever collect paintings, this is the kind I want. Perry Miller thought he was Ahab or wished he was, I thought he was rather mad, he probably thought me the over-fastidious child of privilege if he happened to think of me at all, but between his world and mine there turned out to be an overlap: I think I know something now about the subject of his most famous book, the New England mind. In the presence of Joseph Moore and his family, stiff and staring out of the past, came stirrings of old selves and other lives.

American art by unschooled painters and carvers and quilters and scrimshanders and others was for a long time badly served by its devotees and still hasn't found the perfectly right, intuitive interpreter of its peculiar genius. I'm not that person, though I would like to be, but I'm certain of some things that this curious and difficult-to-name art is not:

it is not decorative or colorful or quaint, however much it delights in ornament, or at least it isn't ever only these things and sometimes isn't any of them. These descriptions are condescensions, usually unconscious, of the well-meaning, but they lead to violations such as that of the more than modestly famous designer who at one point took to cutting up old quilts for I forget what designer purpose. What is decorative, colorful, quaint, may as well be sliced up to serve the needs of the decorator, so the thinking goes. High fashion is high art; naive art or folk art or primitive art, as it was sometimes called before primitive art came to mean only that of tribal cultures, falls too easily though inaccurately into decorator categories. Several decades ago a student of the American scene wrote a book called *The Artist in American Society*, never mentioning, except once in passing in the preface, Edward Hicks or Erastus Salisbury field or Ammi Phillips or Ruth Bascom or any other of the artists, including "anonymous," who in the nineteenth century represented "art" to a large segment of American society. The book's author was on the faculty of the University of Chicago, where popular culture didn't have and never has had much of a following (think of Allan Bloom), except as the province of a learned social anthropology. On American art by the unschooled, real work still waits to be done.

One of the difficulties, tiresome but persistent, has been what to call it. Art "by the unschooled" is ungainly and not even precisely accurate: Erastus Salisbury Field, for example, was briefly apprenticed to Samuel F. B. Morse, a painter in Manhattan before he was an inventor. "Primitive" and "naive" won't do because the work is neither "primitive," even in its sense of original, nor generally "naive," for it often lacks innocence entirely. "Outsider art" refers mostly to work of the deranged or the dispossessed. And calling the whole body of work "folk art" causes trouble because, while quilters and scrimshanders and the dispossessed may be artists of the folk, the New York and New England limners would have some trouble qualifying, and those whose portraits they painted–tough-minded sea captains or doctors and merchants from the aspiring middle and professional class–don't even come close. Folklorists guard the term "folk art" for its ideological tonalities and dismiss the limners, being not of the folk, as unskilled imitators of their artistic betters. Given this difficulty of naming, vernacular art has become the label of last resort, the art of everyday. This label serves well enough except that the neutrality in the idea of the vernacular risks losing sight of particulars that make the art what it is. Myself, I keep on calling it folk art. Who really wants to collect "vernacular art"? But I also prefer not to worry very much about the name. When I studied art history, I had a tough time remembering what was mannerist, what was baroque, what was rococo.

In the American romance, as Miller pointed out, blonde heroines and dark heroines were paired against each other, the one representing dreams of purity and innocence; the other, the threat of the wilderness without that the settlers found on their first coming and the deeper wilderness within. The typology comes from Sir Walter Scott but so well represents the dividedness of American experience as to have become a commonplace, others having followed where Miller led. On the one hand, ours is the promised land, William Bradford's city on a hill, Utopia. On the other, it's a landscape of isolation, violence, death, and more lately urban decay, a haunted scene full of danger. On the one hand, our Utopia is the pastoral green world, Wendover as it was for me; on the other, it is either jagged and sere or else a thick wilderness like the woods that surrounded and hemmed in Wendover's boarding house; and in either case is the setting for Gothic dramas of inner space. (I sense John Finley's ghost again: he was notorious for "on the one hand-ing" and "on the other hand-ing," and undergraduate parodies of him fastened on the gestures that accompanied his division of things, sheep-like and goat-like, into Athenians and Spartans, Greeks and Trojans, scholars and gentlemen.) David Smith's sparseness and his stark sculpture come from the landscape of fear. Ornament is more the style of Utopia. Ornament is also more the style of the gentleman, sparseness that of the scholar, at least in the idealized version of the scholar as votary. Might the double business, to which I have sometimes seemed like Hamlet bound, be American business after all? Not exclusively American business but often so?

Of course the pastoral green world knows death, too: *et in Arcadia ego* says death's voice from beyond the grave; even in Arcady, there I am. The pastoral world merely registers death's presence in a different way from that of the Gothic. Soon after I had fallen heir to the slice of George Bliss's fortune that helped make collecting possible, I bought two versions of a famous nineteenth-century scene, Washington's tomb at Mount Vernon. When the tomb was moved to a location below the plantation house overlooking Chesapeake Bay, a Currier and Ives version of the scene spawned countless imitations. Nothing could better mark American dividedness than my Mount Vernons. One is Mount Vernon as a new Arcady, where death is swallowed up in a burst of pastels, blues and whites and pinks and greens, all shading into each other and figuring the annual resurrection of spring. The other, in charcoal on what is usually referred to as sandpaper but is really board coated with marble dust, figures a paradise lost or missing, a place where the grave and its dark sexuality *are* the goal. The garden is a Gothic fantasy, the phallic tower of the house matching the phallic gazebo; this is Castle Mount Vernon, sinister but alluring. We'd love to know what goes on behind all those blacked-out windows. In the spring sunlight of the pastoral version nothing is hidden or difficult of access: the steps to the house are broad, the ascent gradual, the path between the steps and the gazebo well-traveled. In the Gothic version, the approach to the house, once one has breached the outer walls, is difficult. The lawn looks like a rock formation, the steps look fragile and oddly detached or detachable from the house itself, almost like a drawbridge that could be raised at any time. Commerce between people here is absent, the boats that sail the bay are indistinct and set on their different ways. The industrious little paddle wheeler of the other Mount Vernon, with its secure sense of destination, would be out of place. Here everything is threatening, seductive, silent. Yet Arcadian sunlight is not wholly missing: sparkles of the marble dust glint and glitter through, though they hardly show in reproduction. The green world and the Gothic world are reciprocal, on the one hand and on the other.

Why buy a painting, this one rather than that? Why the two Mount Vernons? Buying a piece of art has the feeling of submitting to necessity, even when part of the truth may be that some dealer knows your need, or "need," better than yourself. Still, you have to make the need your own. That is what the circling of the quarry, the tics and hesitations, the taking on approval, and then the final acceptance are all about. The two Mount Vernons weren't what the art world calls important pictures, but folk art yields importance in unexpected places. My belated perception of the paintings as a double-faced emblem goes to prove, if proof were required, that importance lies where you find it and that you may feel it before you understand it, that the sense of submitting to the necessary may have been grounded in something real.

Sometimes, though, you don't have to hesitate. As Emily Dickinson (or someone) said, "I know it's art if I feel like it takes the top of my head off." Two other paintings, more certifiably important than the two Mount Vernons, just about took the top of my head off: the one, Erastus Salisbury Field's night piece of the Israelites crossing the Red Sea; the other, Ammi Phillips's portrait, by now an American icon, of a little girl in a blazing red dress with her cat and dog. Each fits neatly into the American drama of light confronting dark. But when I saw them first, abstractions like the American drama were far from my thoughts. I was driven by desire, a craving to capture the one thing needful.

Each time, success was a matter of luck, of being in the right place, with enough money, at the right time. Stories of the big one that got away are fishermen's currency, like that of the novice angler in Alaska who hooked a gigantic salmon, perhaps the hundred-pounder the fishing world was waiting for, fought it day and night for thirty-six hours, and finally brought it to the surface, only to let the rod tip down at the last moment and watch his prize swim away. Stories of the big one that didn't get away are collectors' currency, no doubt because the prize is on the wall and yielding its pleasures, unless of course if it turns out to be a fake, in which case it becomes an object lesson rather than a satisfaction. I have had a couple of pieces that may have been fakes and a few more from which I now tend to avert my thought though they still please the eye: one year in London I bought some Greek and Russian icons that, if genuine, were certainly smuggled from somewhere, and they make me uncomfortable now, rather like a stuffed trout or the Elgin marbles, because neither the icons nor the trout nor the marbles are quite where they should be. This is why the fish that got away is if anything more satisfying than the one that didn't and the painting that didn't get away, provided it turns out to be, as connoisseurs say, "right," more satisfying than the one that did. In the collector's mind the painting that didn't get away has found its proper home.

Erastus Salisbury Field lived for nine-five years, from 1805 to 1900, working mostly in the Connecticut River valley. He was the only one of the folk portraitists to keep on painting after photography arrived at mid-century. His livelihood as a portraitist having been taken away, he turned gamely to other subjects: among them, the huge and spectacular "Historical Monument of the American Republic," nine feet by thirteen, which now covers an entire wall in the Springfield Museum of Fine Arts, and a series of paintings, taken from prints and paintings by the English visionary John Martin, illustrating the plagues of Egypt and intended as decoration for a church in North Amherst. Nine of the series are known to have survived, several of them depicting events before and during the Exodus, including "The Israelites Crossing the Red Sea." As late as 1984, it was one of only two not in a museum, though in time it will be. But I knew none of this when I saw it advertised by a dealer from Long Island whom I'd not heard of but who later became a friend. All I knew was that here was a sublimely spooky picture beckoning from the pages of the magazine *Antiques*. The trouble was, the magazine arrived on the West coast days after it arrived in the mailbox of Eastern collectors who I thought would surely have landed the prize. But they hadn't and with a phone call I did. I still wonder why no one else got there first. Maybe it was because the Eastern collectors were all on holiday in Palm Beach, maybe because religious paintings are not in favor, maybe it really was just supposed to be. The stars shone on the venture. And, because part of the allure of collecting comes with the feeling of having acquired a bargain, I will say what it cost: a trifling $3,000, trifling at least compared to its worth today.

The stars shone even brighter a few years later. A traveling show, "The Flowering of American Folk Art," had come to San Francisco in the summer of 1974, and I had seen Phillips's little girl for the first time, her snow-white cat in her arms, a motley dog at her feet, four strands of coral around her neck, dark eyes and pink skin and reddish hair, and the look of an infant Mona Lisa, innocence all tangled up with prescient knowledge. I was captivated by her and also by the credit line: she was "privately owned." If so, then maybe she wasn't forever out of reach, and a collector more entrepreneurial than I might have been on the phone the next day. Yet I don't believe that imaginary entrepreneur would have taken the prize, even if he–or she, collectors of American folk art have often been women, Abby Aldrich Rockefeller being among the first and best of them–had been able to locate the owner. Watch and wait is often the best strategy.

I first learned the virtues of watching and waiting in another context. In London, late in the 1960s, I happened on a seventeenth-century volume, John Dryden's (and others') translations of Juvenal and Persius, containing some manuscript verses, obscene passages that failed to find their way into Dryden's published version of Juvenal's sixth satire, written out on one of its end pages. I wanted the book badly, both because buried treasure is exciting and because I specialized in the seven-teenth- and eighteenth-century satirists. But the bookseller on whose shelves I found it hated to sell what he had: the more interesting the material, the less he wanted to sell it, and this material was very inter-esting. He said he wanted "to do something with it." Nothing so vulgar as a price for his books was anywhere to be seen, so I was sure the wrong thing to say would be "how much?" As I left his shop on an early summer day, headed home to California, I said I'd write him and did so annually for several years. Finally I tired of the game and wrote once more, saying that if he really didn't want to sell the volume, would he be willing to transcribe the verses and I'd send them on to the editors who were then working on a volume of Dryden's translations? His an-swer came back that, "under the circumstances," maybe it was easiest just to sell me the volume if, that is, I was willing to pay the absurdly low price (another bargain) that he quoted. Euphoric, I cabled back: yes. Unimpressed by cables, the bookseller shipped the volume by sur-face mail to California where it arrived several months later after its passage, I liked to imagine, through the Panama Canal. It was worth having been patient. The verses, while not (it turned out) the only man-uscript copy, added to our knowledge of Dryden and also added a word to the English lexicon: namely, "rubster," meaning "dildo." Though pa-tience goes against my natural grain, this was proof of its usefulness. In time things sometimes just come to you, like the "Girl in Red."

I was sitting on the porch of my house talking with the dealer who had sold me "Crossing the Red Sea." He and his wife had come on a winter vacation to visit their son in California. It was February or March, when easterners come west to visit their sons. And I heard myself say without having planned to, "I don't suppose you know who owns the "Girl in Red," to which James Abbe replied in his understated way, "Yes, my sister-in-law." I said something fatuous: "Really?" And then, "Well, if she ever decides to sell, let me know." In April a note from Kathryn Abbe reported that her sister had "no thought of parting with her red girl," but there comes a moment, I was to find, when it seems impossible not to sell, the moment when you know you have something on your hands you can't afford, in every sense, to keep, above all because the thing has come to seem too much, even if it is too much of a good thing.

When James Abbe let me know, not long after, that the "Girl in Red" was for sale, I didn't hesitate, though the price was more than double anything I'd ever paid for a piece of art before, was in fact almost half what I'd paid for the house I was living in, and even though the market collapse of 1974, a divorce, and the inflation of the 1970s had not improved the state of my resources. But how could I resist? Here was the prize, the one painting that was needful, even the painting that might make more collecting unnecessary. That turned out to be the case. In its coming and subsequent going, the "Girl in Red" put an end to one collector's obsession.

Owning the painting was a heady experience. Only six months after it came to California, it went back to the Whitney Museum in New York for another show and was reproduced in countless postcards and posters. Later the poster decorated the front hallway of Jeremy Irons's house in the closing scenes of the film of John Fowles's *The French Lieutenant's Woman* (1981). For the opening at the Whitney, there was the usual gala with lenders, trustees, collectors, and other dignitaries. My new wife, Brigitte, sat next to Philip Johnson, who said modestly, when asked, "I'm an architect," provoking a dreadful shock of recognition. Through it all, I experienced the same old doubleness. On the one hand, this was happening five or six blocks from where I grew up; I belonged here. On the other hand, I had gone to California twenty years before. On another New York occasion at about the same time as the Whitney opening, a Harvard fund-raising event in the medieval hall of the Metropolitan Museum, I found myself talking with the daughter of a celebrated composer and songwriter. She was a New Yorker, as if by profession, and made it clear I had committed an indiscretion or worse when I lit out for the territories. Once you've left New York, you aren't a New Yorker any more. Of all the places you can't go home to, New York heads the list. At the Whitney opening, as at the Metropolitan, I felt myself an outsider even though 740 Park was a few blocks away.

When the show was over, I decided not to bring the "Girl in Red" home to California. She had grown too visible and too valuable, and the idea of hanging her again on the wall of a not very secure house made me nervous. What if something happened to her, say, a fire, or if she were stolen? It would be my fault for not taking good care of her, and I would be forever known as the one who let her be lost to the world. I didn't want the responsibility. So I loaned her to the Rockefeller collection in Williamsburg where she grew more famous still. When several years passed and it was clear she had left my life for good, someone turned up (anonymity was a condition) who was willing both to pay the right price and to promise that in time the painting would go to the Museum of American Folk Art. That is when I found myself having–which is to say, "having"–to sell, even though I had intended all of the collection to be given away and none of it ever sold. The price was eight times what I'd paid, and since the "Girl in Red" would end up in a museum, I felt I had done right by her. When for years I spent summers in a house on Martha's Vineyard (until the Vineyard filled to overflowing with celebrities, traffic, and the richest of the rich), I sometimes thought of her because she helped pay for it. But when I watched a video of *The French Lieutenant's Woman* to make sure memory wasn't playing false and I saw the girl in her red dress flash quickly on and off the screen, I felt the loss. The painting had been on my wall for half a year, coming and going, it seemed, almost as fast as the image in the film. It was hard to believe it had ever been there at all.

But it had been and "Crossing the Red Sea" still is. Yet both have come to seem less like trophies, aesthetic adornments (however transient in the case of the "Girl in Red") of a comfortable life, than like pieces in the American mosaic. "Crossing the Red Sea" is fantastic, hallucinatory; the "Girl in Red," an image of childhood innocence. The one is sublime, the other beautiful. But look closer and you see convergent combinations of sparseness and ornament, the darkness of their ground and their spasms of brightness, markers in the tradition (and the melodrama) of American romance.

The Israelites in "Crossing the Red Sea" are sublimely beyond numbering, merging with the deep blue background and fading off into the indistinctness of infinitude. Cattle and sheep lead the procession, dream animals thrusting their way into mental spaces beyond illumination from the pillar of fire that follows. Strange spectral figures loom up behind the animals, perhaps the residue of a false start. And, as if in an impossible reflection, the pillar of fire, yellow, pink, and green, is duplicated faintly, half-size, on the middle left of the painting, also perhaps a false start but lending a sense of the surreal, a small hint of Magritte or de Chirico. Yet for all the strangeness, the Israelites are traveling through darkness to freedom and the promised land of milk and honey, a land that is here, beyond the painting, with us. We are the promised land and in it, too. And the promise of the promised land seems forecast in the pinkness of the dotted stars and of the waters falling down the parted sides of the Red Sea. These are the lights of faerie, a choice inspired by the invisible hand of some celestial painter. Surely Field didn't stop to ask himself whether the stars should be white or yellow, pink or blue? Surely he just chose the pink because it was at hand and was right? The pinkness of the stars against the deep sky is the brightness of the American drama shining through, like that of the Israelites' march to freedom. The stars match the gleams and glints of the marble dust in the dark Mount Vernon.

As for the "Girl in Red," what innocence and clarity yet what premonitions, too. Unencumbered by the world, the girl is alone with her pets. The brilliant scarlet of the dress and the whiteness of the cat blare luminously out of the painting as if in a Russian suprematist abstraction. Subtract the girl and the dog and the cat, leave the red and the white, and it could be Malevich. But for all the blaze of color and pattern, for all the tranquillity of her innocence, the girl is a shut-in, posed against a backdrop of somber brown. In John Crowe Ransom's elegiac "Bells for John Whiteside's Daughter" the poet imagines the dead girl as being in a "brown study" that "astonishes us all." In a sophomore English class the instructor assigned us to write an explication of the poem, but I'd never heard of a brown study, and if anybody else in the class had, they weren't telling. Nor did the instructor give any clues, which I thought rather churlish of him when we were all penalized for not having found out, as we could have in any dictionary had it crossed anyone's mind that so metaphorical a phrase could be a dictionary entry, that a brown study is a deep reverie. According to the *Oxford English Dictionary*, the phrase dates back to 1532. And an ordinary desk dictionary at hand gives an example:"lost in a brown study, she was oblivious to the noise." Men could once get lost in brown studies, but now perhaps it is more often women. The serious little girl in red, cradling her cat as a mother would a child, is one of them.

The stiffness of folk portraiture has been criticized for depriving its subjects of lifelikeness. But the rigor of death, foreshadowed here in the girl's stiffened pose, is what portraiture has often been about. We no longer mummify the dead, like the Egyptians, nor paint their images on wood or cloth as in the mummy portraits from the Fayum, nor make death masks like those of Johnson and Keats, nor do we often photograph the dead on their biers or in their coffins, but the tradition of representing the dead is very old, and there are even signs in contemporary art and photography of a revival. Is there the faintest chance that the girl in red is a posthumous portrait? Almost certainly not, but death is in Arcadia: the limner's technique catches the ever-presence of death-in-life like early photographic portraits that required the subject to stay immovably in place for a long, painful time. The pastoral Utopia of Mount Vernon houses Washington's grave. Shepherds gaze at the legend on the tomb in Arcady. And Phillips's little girl, deep in her brown study, looks out at us, a beguiling memento of what's to come.

As for collecting, the lust is gone. I think of Reiner Klimke again and his wonderful horse Ahlerich: I'll never need another "Girl in Red"–a good thing, because I couldn't afford her anyway.

How I Found Uncle Fred–2

Some people are drawn to the margins, often to the North, like Johnson to the Hebrides–or like me. For us, islands have a special lure. They are at the margin of continents (islands in the middle of a lake or river don't really count) and if they're small, you can easily get to their shores. I have been to the outer Hebrides, to rocky Inishmore in the Aran Islands, to Admiralty Island off the coast of Alaska, where Brigitte and I looked in on a Russian Orthodox ceremony at a church in Angoon, the westernmost point of the island. But others prefer the interior, often the tropics, Africa or the Amazon–like the artist Tobias Schneebaum, who took his Fulbright to Brazil and instead of painting went deep and then deeper into the jungle. He wrote a book about his journey, and its title could be the legend for any journey to the interior: *Keep the River on Your Right.* I read him with fascination though not with any conscious longing to follow. Deciding to track Uncle Fred to the middle of Africa therefore meant an unfamiliar sort of journey. Perhaps the ghost of Mungo Park, the eighteenth-century lowland Scot who traveled in East Africa at repeated and great risk, haunts me unawares.

Brigitte and I had been to Africa before, tourists in the Serengeti like thousands of others, gawking at a giant martial eagle high on a tree in Ngorogoro crater, listening to Swahili carols sung on Christmas Eve by

24.

25.

24.
Wendover, 1914, Alman & Co., NYC

25.
Wendover burning, Nov. 8, 1979,
Bernardsville (NJ) News

26.

27.

28.

29.

30.

26.
WBC and tree, ca. 1934

27.
WBC as a child-soldier in the
Knickerbocker Greys, ca. 1940

28.
WBC in Buckley School uniform,
sitting on Wendover steps, 1937

29.
Sibyll Bliss Carnochan with WBC,
ca. 1932, studio photo, Walter Scott
Shinn, NYC

30.
WBC at the grave of George Bliss,
Greenwood Cemetery, Brooklyn,
NY, ca. 1996

31.
Brigitte Carnochan in Livingstone's
house, Tabora, Tanzania, 1995,
photo by WBC

31.

32.

33.

34.

35.

32.
Fred Carnochan in uniform, ca.
1918, studio photo, Pirie MacDon-
ald, "Photographer of Men," NYC

33.
Fred Carnochan and his brother
Gouv, ca. 1896, studio photo,
"Barker," Yonkers, NY

34.
Site of initiation into Porcupine
Guild, 1934, photo by F. G.
Carnochan, The Explorers
Club, NYC.

35.
Site of initiation into Snake Guild,
1934, photo by F. G. Carnochan, The
Explorers Club, NYC.

36.

37.

38.

36.
WBC, Simon Sitta (left), and village elders, Mawere Shamba, Tanzania 1995, photo by Brigitte Carnochan

37.
Simon Sitta, Shinyanga, Tanzania, 1995, photo by Brigitte Carnochan

38.
Kitanga Mali Fesa, Mawere Shamba, Tanzania, 1995, photo by Brigitte Carnochan

39.

39.
"The Israelites Crossing the Red
Sea", ca. 1865-70, oil on canvas,
Erastus Salisbury Field

40.
"Mt. Vernon", ca. 1838, pastel on
board, anonymous, University of
California, Berkeley Art Museum

41.
"Mt. Vernon", ca. 1840, pastel on
paper, anonymous, University of
California, Berkeley Art Museum

40.

41.

42.

42.
"Girl in Red Dress with Cat and
Dog," ca. 1830-35, oil on canvas,
Ammi Phillips, Museum of Ameri-
can Folk Art, NYC, promised
anonymous gift.

the choir of the Ngorogoro Methodist church, and overhearing one of our fellow tourists whispering loudly into the recording device of his camcorder to tell his audience back home what they would be seeing, for example, "two lions copulating in the Serengeti." This trip had been a riskless way to see if I really wanted to try to track down Uncle Fred. When Africa worked its spell, I decided I could attempt the interior, not least because Brigitte–the resilient offspring not of privilege but of a life-journey from Germany, when she was six, to Beloit, Wisconsin, then to Fort Worth, Texas, then to high school in Fontana, California, home of the original Hell's Angels, eventually to an English Ph.D. from Berkeley and finally to a career in photography–would come with me. What I really decided was that the two of us could do it.

Short of starting life over, I knew I couldn't become a proficient student of Africa and the Wanyamwesi, but help is seldom far away at a university because there is always someone who knows something about whatever you may want to know. Through Stanford's linguistics department, I located the young Wanyamwesi-born student and small shop owner–he eked out a living selling African fabrics and knick-knacks–who lived in East Palo Alto, who read Fred's book, and who said he was a brave man. I talked to Yassini often, thought I might try to learn something of his language, wrote a letter to his brother, a botanist at the University of Dar es Salaam, asking if he would be willing to act as a guide, got a reply a year later (saying yes), only to discover one day that Yassini had pulled up stakes for I didn't know where. I decided I needed to find someone else who knew their way about East Africa.

The academic grapevine had the answer. An African historian at Stanford put me in touch with another African historian, visiting for a year, who was married to a Ph.D. student in anthropology who had done her field work near Lake Tanganyika and who knew another American student working in Shinyanga (on the main road north from Tabora) and studying African languages with a secondary schoolteacher whose name was Simon Sitta. So I wrote Denise Roth in Shinyanga, phoned her on the day and at the time she suggested in her reply, and followed her advice to get in touch with Simon, a member of the Wasukuma, the largest of more than 100 tribes in Tanzania, with some 6,000,000 people and a language closely related to Nyamwesi, as American is to English. Without Simon Sitta's help, there would be no story to tell here. I sent him an extra copy of Fred's book that a dealer in Africana had found for me, we corresponded regularly, and two years later settled on a day when we'd all meet in Tabora, I with my notebook, Brigitte with her camera, and Simon with whatever knowledge he had acquired of Uncle Fred and of the snake men.

When Stanley set out to find Livingstone (who was never really "lost") in 1871, the flamboyant Scot James Gordon Bennett, editor of the *New York Herald* and sponsor of Stanley's trip, asked how much it would cost. Stanley said not less than £2,500 and Bennett replied: "'Well, I will tell you what you will do. Draw a thousand pounds now; and when you have gone through that, draw another thousand, and when that is spent, draw another thousand, and when you have finished that, draw another thousand, and so on; but FIND LIVINGSTONE.'" I didn't have James Gordon Bennett's resources, but thanks to Stanford (the dean agreed this counted as research) and to the posthumous beneficence of George Bliss that had also enabled me to buy the "Girl in Red," we were well provided for. We would not have to rely on African buses for getting around Tanzania.

From San Francisco to Arusha, near Mount Kilimanjaro, by way of Amsterdam takes twenty hours of flying through eleven time zones. We set out on a November day in 1995. There was a light drizzle in Amsterdam and we bought umbrellas. We went to the Rijksmuseum and found "The Night Watch" on the same wall, I thought, where I'd seen it forty years before. There were no Vermeers, for they were on exhibit in Washington. The canals were dotted with yellow leaves. Winter was about to settle in, but it was not cold—luckily, because we had no space in the bags for heavy clothes. After two nights in Amsterdam we took an early-morning cab to the airport and were on our way to Africa.

As we were boarding the plane, an attendant said we would have to check one of our carry-on bags. We argued with her but not forcefully enough. We'd prepared for the possibility by packing the duffel bag with less essential gear and several small cameras for gifts, and at least it would be on the plane with us. We landed at Kilimanjaro at night, there to find that it had stayed on the plane, was on its way to Dar es Salaam, and wouldn't return for at least two days if, I thought, ever. We congratulated ourselves for having planned well and chastised ourselves for not having put up more of a fight with the flight attendant. We were picked up at the airport, spent the night in Arusha, and the next morning were ready to go looking for Fred.

The question had been, how to get to Tabora? The Tanzanian airline was said to own one unreliable plane that flew somewhat irregularly to Tabora from Dar es Salaam. Trains and buses were for hardier and younger tourists, and when we saw the buses jammed with travelers (when they weren't stopped for repairs, as they often were, their passengers squatting or sitting or lying on the ground as they waited), we were happy not to be on one. Instead we had arranged for a driver and a Landcruiser. In the event, and to our surprise, we had not one driver but two: the one, George Makinda, born near Tabora, a Wanyamwesi; the other, Felician Baraza, from the Cushitic tribe of the Iraqw, son of a well-to-do farmer on the outer, southeast slope of Ngorogoro crater, prodigiously learned about East African flora and fauna, and a guide for Prince Charles when he had gone on a Tanzanian safari. George and Felician were sturdy and reassuring, and George responded to questions about risks along the road–we had been regaled at home with others' warnings, quite baseless as it turned out, of bandits and kidnappings–by saying in a tone that hovered between impatience and understanding, "we carry machetes." Why we had two drivers, we never quite knew; but George said, "One of us might get sick." Tabora was off the usual tourist route and we supposed George's and Felician's bosses didn't want to risk trouble. Hotels in Tabora, the travel company was at pains to tell us, were not what their customers were used to. We would have to find a place to stay when we got there ourselves. George, they assured us, knew the territory well.

When Livingstone died, deep in the African interior in May 1873, his servants Chuma and Susi buried his heart and internal organs, covered his body with salt and left it in the sun for two weeks, then with a party of seventy men and women carried it for nine months and 1,400 miles to the sea, there to be returned to England and buried in Westminster Abbey. I thought George and Felician would have done no less, had they been of Livingstone's party. We felt secure with them, and not just because of the machetes. When George said, after the trip was done and we were getting on a plane to Zanzibar (one more island for the lifetime list), "We will miss you," it took any curse off the privilege we had brought with us. We would miss them, too.

Tabora lies 700 kilometers and two days' drive from Arusha, most of the way, Felician warned, on "African roads." The tarmac ended not far outside Arusha, a city whose comparative prosperity and intermittently paved roads come from the flourishing wildlife and tourist industry. Now, as we left Arusha behind, it was all bumping and bouncing and hanging on. For lunch we turned off the road to eat the sandwiches we'd brought with us and soon were surrounded (it is always like this in Africa, but we didn't know it then) by inquisitive boys from neighboring farms who popped up as if they had been camouflaged in the landscape. We spent the first night in Singhida, where a San Francisco acquaintance had recalled from his Peace Corps days the worst hotel of his life. We were happy to find the Singhida "motel" for sixteen dollars a night. A big truck distributing condoms was parked outside, and we had dinner in the garden area, listening in on a disco. Its purpose, George told us, was AIDS prevention. A waitress came over, smiling, but her English was not good and we weren't sure what we'd ordered. It turned out to be, not for the last time, chicken and chips; African chickens have a better life than their cousins from Perdue or Tyson and come to the table less plump, tougher, but with a sort of rugged authenticity. Not only were we in a part of Tanzania tourists don't see, Felician hadn't seen it either. This was his first trip to the middle of the country.

African roads are monotonous. There's no wildlife except in the game parks, and the villages, though full of roadside activity, are indistinguishable from one another. Coming down a long, winding grade on our second day, we saw some small, leafy tree branches on the road and Felician said, "an accident." We understood what he meant as we rounded a steep curve and passed an overturned petrol truck. No one was hurt, but the truck might have blocked our way for hours or days, had we and the truckers, who sat stoically waiting for help, been less lucky. By evening we were in Tabora, a town of maybe 10,000, with churches, mosques, inns, a sports stadium, and the bustle of every African town. The day before, George had made arrangements, not an easy thing to do on Tanzania's archaic telephone system, to meet Simon Sitta at the Golden Eagle lodge. When we found it, it looked unpromising. The rooms and bar and dining room were on the second floor, and going up the dingy stairwell I wondered if we would find Simon there. He was waiting in the outdoor lobby as if he had been there always, a slightly built man, perhaps fifty, with graying hair and not very good teeth. We smiled a welcome to each other. Our room cost eight dollars a night. It was lit by a single bulb, had a private bathroom but no hot water, and a wardrobe with three condoms on a shelf. When we couldn't suppress a look of faint reluctance, Simon shook his head: "It's the best hotel in Tabora." We decided we were were willing to take his word for it.

Simon lives and teaches in Lalago, about two hundred kilometers and eight hours by bus from Tabora. When I wrote him first, I didn't understand African distances: on the map Lalago is near Shinyanga which is near Tabora. Looking at the map, I didn't realize how much time, energy, and persistence would be required when I asked Simon if he would help me track down "Kalola" and Fred. He wrote back and said, "I trust and respect Denise and therefore will not let you down." And he proposed to get to work right away:"I think we have time to level the ground." The reason he said yes, I came to believe, was not so much because I would pay him as because he liked the idea. He has written a biography of a medicine man who lived in Mwanza at the turn of the century, and he said to me once, "We don't mind our heroes. They live and they pass away and that's the end of it." Simon believes in heroes and would not understand the western world's fall into mock-heroic. He also has the historian's passion for digging up the past. What western historians do in libraries, archives, and public record offices, he does in the dusty villages of central Africa. But until we met and events unfolded, I had little idea of how much he had done or with what success.

I only knew that Mawere Shamba was south of Tabora and that we were nearby. Going there required a permit and also a preparatory visit by Simon to let the villagers know we were coming. On our first morning, George and Simon went to find the official who would issue the permit, but it was raining, the official had no car, and hadn't come to work. He would be in later, "bado kidogo." Having been told that the White Fathers—the Society of Missionaries of Africa, whose outposts are all over the continent—keep good historical records, we drove to their compound at Kipalapala Seminary, a few kilometers south of Tabora. We discovered no archives, which later turned out to be in Tabora itself and contained no hint of Fred or snakes, but found ourselves in the midst of a jubilee celebrating the opening of a printing press at the mission fifty years before. We had seen women in festive clothes walking on the road and now we knew where they had been going. A service was in progress, men on one side of the church, women and children on the other, and a chorus of ululating voices, exotic to western ears. There was a break for lunch, and in the afternoon, a carnival:

dancing, drumming, acrobatics, singing, in the shade of overhanging trees. One of the White Fathers, not in clerical dress, stood on the edge of the crowd with his camcorder and cheerfully answered our questions about who was who and what was happening. Some spectators, mostly children, climbed the trees to look on, but the places of honor were for the Archbishop of Tabora, the Bishop of Kigoma, and a local Benedictine abbot, all in gleaming white robes, unsullied by the dust; the robes of the Archbishop and the Bishop had pink and fuchsia trimmings. There is talk of an African Pope sometime soon. To an onlooker from the West, African Christianity has the feel of being unselfconsciously the real thing.

Simon had his spadework to do in Mawere Shamba, and in the afternoon he and George took the Landcruiser, leaving us with Felician at the jubilee. One of the dancers, an old woman we'd seen earlier on the road, was reluctant to smile for a photograph because she had so few teeth but was in such good spirits that not smiling was impossible and she broke into a broad grin at her own reluctance. Another celebrant, a young man of about twenty, sat down beside me and said in good English, "Are you going to teach me English?" When I came home, I sent him Maya Angelou's account of her years in Ghana and Norman McLean's *A River Runs Through It*. He wrote back saying his father had died so now he couldn't pay for school and would I send him money to buy a car? Late in the afternoon, we took a taxi back to town. I was tired and turned down the chance to see Tabora play a soccer game against a neighboring town. Later I was sorry I hadn't gone, though I learned Tabora had lost.

The rain had stopped and the official who issued permits showed up at the hotel in a very dark suit. The next morning, permit in hand, we set out again on the road south, past the White Fathers, past a house where Livingstone had lived that was now a museum (to which only a young villager possessed the key), "bumping along over rather rugged country" (Fred's words), and eventually stopping at the village of Pangale, just off the road, where a small crowd of adults and children had gathered. Among them were three old men, two of them probably in their seventies, each with a serene dignity; the third was a small man, certainly in his eighties, withered by age. Simon introduced us and said, gesturing toward one of the younger two, "That is the son of Mali Fesa." It was breathtaking. I had had no idea what was in store. Could I actually be shaking hands with the son of the man who stood proxy for Fred Carnochan and therefore shared his soul? And if all this were true, could something of heart and spirit have joined us across years and continents? The Stanley-Livingstone melodrama, for all its journalistic contrivance, suddenly made sense as an allegory of finding the familiar at the heart of a remote world, meaning incarnate in the interior. The three old men crowded into the Landcruiser with us and we headed deeper into the back country. On the way we talked about Fred.

"He was famous," they said. "He was courageous." "He was tall," said the son of Mali Fesa, "like you," which in fact he wasn't but instead short and stocky and ill-suited to climbing down porcupine holes. When the son of Mali Fesa knew Fred, however, the old man would have been in his early teens at the oldest and probably younger, and I told myself, ever needing to maintain conviction, that just as the middle-aged seem old to the young, the not-so-tall seem taller than they really are. And as the tales continued, Fred turned into legend, a student not only of Kalialia's and of good snake-medicine but also of Kalialia's rival, Wakaluma the sorcerer, from whom he learned something of witchcraft. Wakaluma's name never appears in *The Empire of the Snakes*, and I wondered if he might be the Porcupine-man whose name Fred is at pains to say he has forgotten. In the Carnochan-Adamson *Out of Africa* is a long appendix with notations on guilds and local customs. One of the entries, headed "Black Magic Guild–Lozi," reports that "there is continued warfare between the priestly mutanda," or lodges, "and the sorcerers" known as "lozi." And though "the whole group of Lozi is nebulous and hard to find, … it definitely exists and under proper auspices the gatherings may be witnessed." What the proper auspices might be, Fred never lets on, but he describes some Lozi ceremonies and medicines. Evidently he did know something about the sorcerers' craft and felt he had to handle the subject carefully. The Wanyamwesi are proficient in witchcraft and sorcery, and one anthropologist reported in the 1960s that "the most renowned witch" he encountered in Ukaguru, southeast of Tabora, "was a Nyamwezi whose intelligence and boldness enabled him to inspire respect and build up an extensive counter-witchcraft and alleged poison trade. By his unusual dress and fierce bearing"–a description that would serve for Kalialia, too, whose royal regalia included not only a green hat with leopard skin and an ostrich feather but also the leather belt of a German soldier that still read, faintly, "Gott Mit Uns"–"he took great pains to encourage this belief."

As we jounced along the narrow road through the forest from Pangale to Mawere Shamba, this is the story we were told. When Fred returned on his last visit, another of Kalialia's students had died, strangely: deaths in Africa, especially if they are in any way out of the ordinary, are often thought to have been caused by witchcraft. And Kalialia, too, Fred was told, had died not of natural causes but of Wakaluma's magic, for Wakaluma was jealous of Kalialia's having taken a "European" as a student. Wakaluma told Fred, however, "Kalialia is not dead," and the two of them climbed a hill where Fred saw Kalialia and called out to him. When Kalialia didn't answer, Wakaluma said, "We have cut out his tongue." And Fred broke into tears. Then in the night, Wakaluma took Fred on a spirit ride to America. The next morning they were back in Mawere Shamba. Soon Fred left for home and never returned because, despite his bravery, he feared Wakaluma and his witchcraft. Then as the story ended, the Landcruiser came to a stop in another tiny village, George showed our permit to the village schoolmaster, and I thought, "So this is Mawere Shamba." But it wasn't: it was a village called Igigwa. We got out and started walking, following the old men, we weren't sure to where.

After a kilometer or so, the three began pointing to one place or another: "Fred lived there," "Kalialia lived here," "Nyoka lived there." It was while walking across this open space that Simon said, "We don't mind our heroes." But of Mawere Shamba itself, there was no sign; it had gone from the face of the earth, vanished like Fred's inheritance. I had assumed we were headed to where the three old men lived, but no: they lived twenty kilometers away on the other side of the main road, had gotten up at 4:30 in the morning, and had walked to Pangale to meet us. They had not been to Mawere Shamba for forty years. Why they and everyone else had left the village we never learned. George said maybe it had been infected with witchcraft, but rural African villages are impermanent fixtures on the landscape. Perhaps the soil had grown infertile. Perhaps the soil had grown infertile because of witchcraft. Mali Fesa's son looked for the place where his father's house had stood and where he had been born. Finally, when he found three stones arranged in a rough triangle on the ground, he said this was where the house had been. The stones had been used for grinding meal. We all stood near the stones for picture-taking; they were the closest thing we found to a trace of Mawere Shamba.

On the way back, we stopped just short of Pangale and got out of the Landcruiser to say our good-byes without the crowd of villagers around. I made a little speech of thanks and friendship that Simon didn't translate, though I had wanted him to. Awkwardly I gave the old men a thousand shillings apiece (a couple of dollars) and Simon said, "I thought you were going to privilege Mali Fesa," surprising me with a verb more common in literary theory, I'd have thought, than in Tanzanian English. I gave Kitanga Mali Fesa, as was his full name, another thousand shillings, feeling more awkward than ever. We drove off and watched the three of them standing in the middle of the road, watching us silently. I remembered what I'd said to myself about this trip, so long in the planning: that if I were to find Uncle Fred, it had better be now, or soon, or not ever.

The adventure was not quite over. At Pangale the crowd was still gathered along with, it turned out, one villager who had not been present when we passed through earlier nor when Simon and George had been there the day before. The man came over to the car. He was upset and talked heatedly to George through the front window. His name was Omari Salum. He said he was Nyoka's grandson and had learned the secrets of snake-catching from his grandfather. He was angry because he had wanted to show me his skill and angry also because the elders, other than Mali Fesa, had no connection with the Snakes. George replied to him evenly. Brigitte and I sat a little nervously in the back seat until we drove off, having used the oldest of evasions, "next time"; the next time we were in Pangale, Omari Salum and I would go looking for snakes. Sometimes, when things go wrong for what seems the sake of going wrong, I wonder, not wholly in jest, if I have been cursed by Omari Salum.

As we drove away, I had another surge of doubtfulness: could all this have been staged? For the money and for the candy we gave the children of Pangale? Surely that was impossible? Yet months after I came home I read an anthropologist's comment that the first "invariable" rule of fieldwork is that "most informants lie most of the time," and I suffered still another seizure of uncertainty. Still it's less credible that the three old men were lying than that they were telling what they thought was true. Embellishing, probably; lying, no. The time comes to put suspicion aside, if only out of plain weariness. Is the anthropologist's first rule of fieldwork not just one more imposition that whites have laid on indigenous peoples?

The next day we went to Usoke, another of Kalialia's dwelling places, a mostly Arab town west of Tabora where Simon had followed Fred's trail. First he had consulted a medicine man in Tabora who had told him of another old man in Usoke who had known Kalialia. But the old man in Usoke had been dead for three years. Only after other false leads and much walking about did Simon discover a man in Usoke who told him how to find Mawere Shamba. Simon is blessed not only with a researcher's instincts but, just as important for seekers after obscure knowledge, with good luck. To retrace some of his footsteps was to relive the exhilarations of searching and at last of finding.

It had all happened very fast. The next day we were back on the road, headed three hundred kilometers north to Mwanza, where Fred had been the object of so much perhaps-not-wholly-unwelcome attention. The rains, having just begun, had not yet watered down the dry uplands, and the landscape was harsh and arid, like the interior valleys of California in September. For lunch we drove into a dry, open field, parked beside a giant baobab tree (big enough to retire modestly behind in order to take care of our physical needs) and ate mangoes and tinned sardines served, as usual, off a blanket on the hood of the Landcruiser. After lunch we stopped in Jomu, hoping to meet Simon's daughter, a schoolteacher like her father. But complications of a pregnancy had taken her to Shinyanga for medical care. At her school we were engulfed in scrubbed and noisy schoolchildren in uniform, both boys and girls, who rushed to meet and greet us, jumping up and down to see over the heads of their fellows, though the schoolmaster made them keep a distance. We stopped in Shinyanga, but no one was at the small shack-like house where Simon's son lived and where his daughter, he assumed, was staying. We took farewell pictures of each other sitting together on a bench outside the house, two at a time. My pictures of Simon and Brigitte were not as good as hers of Simon and me, and we didn't include my efforts in the batch we sent him from California. Months later he wrote and asked to have one of the pictures of Brigitte and him, "for everlasting remembrance." When we said good-bye to Simon, he said, "Go in peace." Driving away, we saw him waiting outside his son's door, just as he waited for us at the Golden Eagle. Later he would take the bus, crowded and rickety no doubt, home to Lalago.

We drove on to Mwanza and coming into town saw a fisherman or middleman wheeling a big cart overflowing with tilapia, the fat, flat-bodied local fish from Lake Victoria. The good hotels were full, and we ended up in a sixteen-dollar-a-night place run by East Indians. Heavy rain pelted the city during the night, and the next morning we had to slosh through inches of water on the bathroom floor, whether from the rain or otherwise we couldn't tell. From Mwanza we headed east, with Speke Gulf (the nineteenth-century explorer John Speke first identified Lake Victoria as the source of the Nile) and the lake to the north, then crossed the Serengeti, passed through the Ngorogoro highlands where we saw the hillside on which Felician's father had grazed his several hundreds of cattle, and three days after leaving Mwanza arrived in Arusha where we had started fourteen hundred kilometers before and where our errant duffel bag was waiting in the KLM office. With George's help, we shipped the cameras to Simon and his family in Lalago after much tussling with the post office bureaucracy and excessive applications of sealing wax on the package at every intersection of string.

Driving through the Serengeti we had had only a little time for wildlife, though the herds of wildebeest had begun their migration south with the coming of the rainy season, but at one point Felician drove off the main road and we came to a pool of standing water, brilliantly green with algae. In the water were a somnolent hippo and some crocodiles and, stretched out and napping on a rock, a Goliath heron, one of the world's biggest, most majestic birds. On a fishing trip with Kalialia to the Ugala river, west of Tabora, Fred saw a Goliath heron and uncharacteristically stopped in his narrative to note its size and beauty. We only glimpsed the heron briefly yet it made a continuity between Fred's African sojourns and ours.

Fred Carnochan's remains lie in the vault of St. Ann's, Morrisania, along with the other Carnochans and Morrises. He was the last for whom there was any space. At his funeral I was glad to think that when my turn came, I wouldn't have to spend eternity in that claustrophobic setting. When it was built, St. Ann's was a country church. Now it stands in the midst of the poorest congressional district in the country with a population largely African-American and Hispanic, close to 50 percent unemployed or on government aid, and high percentages of

HIV, infant mortality, tuberculosis. Every so often, plaques commemorating one or another of the Morrises are stolen off the church walls. But there are life and energy in the surrounding streets, as in the church itself, a busy parish with a racially mixed congregation of some 400 souls. The street scene resembles that of any African town. For all his privilege, a child of Africa in one of his lives, Fred rests among poverty and the descendants of slaves. I think of this happenstance as intimating a future when the worst inequities of American life might fade away. I also think of the close of Carnochan's *Out of Africa* and his hope that whites might stop exploiting Africa. If that in some sense has happened, it has not been the result of any particular goodwill.

The Minister's Black Veil

Is not one single term repeated enough to break down
and confound the history of the world, to reveal that
there is no such history?
Borges, "A New Refutation of Time"

Having finished the book about Swift that got me tenure in 1968, as it would not today, I found myself writing an essay on Hawthorne's story "The Minister's Black Veil." I "found myself" writing it because subjects seem to discover me as much as *vice-versa*. Somehow things just come along, and "The Minister's Black Veil" was an odd thing to have come along, given my encounter with Perry Miller and my lingering doubt that American literature was worth bothering with. I liked Hawthorne, though, whom I'd first read for Miller and whose novels had been the subject of the paper that made up somewhat for my botched essay on Whitman. My infatuation with American folk art had begun, and "The Minister's Black Veil," a dark representation of the American psyche, mirrored the spookiness of a painting like Field's "Crossing the Red Sea." But writing about it was a sport, not part of any premeditated move from the old world to the new.

One Sunday in New England, the story goes, the Reverend Mr. Hooper, "a gentlemanly person, of about thirty, though still a bachelor" and known for his goodness and piety, comes to meeting wearing a black veil. The townspeople gossip and guess about his reasons, but no one ever learns why he wears the veil, not even the woman he was supposed to marry and certainly not Hawthorne's readers. For all its mysteriousness, however, the veil was not just a product of Hawthorne's imagination; it had a precedent in seventeenth-century New England, as a note that he attaches to the story indicates:

> Another clergyman in New England, Mr. Joseph Moody, of York, Maine, who died about eighty years since, made himself remarkable by the same eccentricity that is here related of the Reverend Mr. Hooper. In his case, however, the symbol had a different import. In early life he had accidentally killed a beloved friend; and from that day till the hour of his own death, he hid his face from men.

This note, I said, doesn't help much. In fact it adds to the puzzlement, explaining no more than one reason why Hooper didn't wear the veil and none why he did. Hawthorne enjoyed teasing readers with false or doubtful leads. This is one of them. Starting the story we know nothing of Hooper's reasons and very little of Moody's. How Moody killed his friend Hawthorne doesn't say–the historical record is that when he was eight he accidentally shot a ten-year-old playmate–nor can we tell whether the veil is a penance or a shame or, as seems to have been the historical case, not even immediately related to the accident. Hawthorne is toying with, not giving, an explanation of Hooper's veil.

My little essay contained no amenities of the factual: no new sources, nothing new about the Reverend Mr. Moody, nothing that might be counted as a discovery. This was unusual: I mistrust interpretation that lacks any trace of external reference. The "new criticism" of the 1940s and 1950s that I grew up with was an intellectual performance of astonishing self-confidence and virtuosity on the part of learned readers who set out single-handedly to wrestle poems to the ground. But who was to referee? Myself, I like having something more to hang an interpretation on, some evidence outside the text: especially–however at odds with the "new critical" way of thinking–biographical understanding. Jack Bate, after all, gave his students Johnson, not a new critical reading of "The Vanity of Human Wishes." But with "The Minister's Black Veil," I was on my own.

It's a mistake, I said, to try to look behind the veil and explain why Mr. Hooper wears it. Not only the townspeople but the critics, most famously Edgar Allan Poe, have guessed at Hooper's reasons. Poe thought Hooper had committed a "crime of dark dye" against a "young lady" whose burial the story describes. It is a vulgar theory, not hinted at in the story. Others have also tried to get at Hooper's motive. But I said the veil works in the way Thomas Carlyle described the working of symbols: they conceal and reveal at the same time. Look under the veil and meaning vanishes. I still think this is right. It's useless to speculate why Hooper put on the veil. Since we can't possibly know, why look for trouble? Sometimes, though, things (like the "Girl in Red") come unbidden. We stumble on primal scenes, we don't seek them out.

By the time I wrote the essay, my mother had died, I'd spent a year in London and then moved into a house in California big enough to accommodate her furniture and the refectory table–in an oak-paneled dining room where with friends we sometimes replicated eighteenth-century dinners–and other of her belongings, including boxes and boxes of documents and photographs out of which some of this story has been made, an intimidating mass of material that I put off looking at for years. When I finally did, I found the clippings about weddings (including the sharp-tongued bitchery of the Club-Fellow); obituary tribute after obituary tribute to forbear after forbear; John Murray Carnochan's surgical textbook and his pamphlet, taken from a public address, on the cerebral localization of insanity; an album of Civil War *cartes de visites*, often signed by generals and admirals on the Union side, Grant and Sherman and Meade and Burnside and others; General William Walton Morris's commissions, one of them signed by Lincoln; a letter concerning Morris's denial of *habeas corpus* at Fort McHenry amidst other letters and still more letters; bibles and still more bibles; genealogies in expensive bindings; *Burke's Landed Gentry* including "American Families with British Ancestry," among them the Carnochans–"formerly of Gatehouse of Fleet"; Katharine Baldwin's dance card at the Yale Senior Promenade in 1892 (she danced with Walter Bliss first, last, and once in the middle of that June evening); my school reports and the phonograph record of me telling the world that when I grew up I wanted to be "an aviator"; and a few documents that reached farther into the past, even some letters from William Farnham, a boy of "great promise" who had gone to Harvard in the

1700s, had died at sixteen, and who was a forbear of Sibyl A. Lambard, the wife-to-be of Governor Henry Porter Baldwin. Amidst this profusion was a notebook, bound in soft red morocco and stamped on the front in gold: FAMILY EPITAPHS. Inside was the signature of Sibyl A. Lambard Baldwin. Someone more knowledgeable could identify the date of the notebook. To my eye it has a nineteenth-century look, as does the idea of transcribing family epitaphs. Yet it might be later: Sibyl Baldwin, born in 1841, didn't die until 1922, outliving her husband the governor by almost thirty years.

What the notebook contains is not family epitaphs but Sibyl Baldwin's transcription (it may be the transcription of a transcription) of a journal and of letters by her great-aunt Katharine Farnham Hay, born in 1751, for whom Katharine Baldwin Bliss may have been named; and, also, of an "introduction" to the journal written by Sibyl Baldwin's aunt Phebe Bliss Farnham Cobb, her mother's twin sister, in about 1825. Katharine Hay's journal and letters recount her experience in 1778 of making her way through the American lines to join her Tory, Scottish husband in New York before embarking with him for London and for safety. But it is Phebe Cobb's "introduction" to Katharine Hay's story, with its brief chronicle of the Farnhams, that tangled me in a web of circumstance.

I have trouble keeping the genealogy straight: it's like trying to remember the names of a friend's children whom you've not met and therefore lack faces with names attached. The genealogy goes backwards, thus: Sibyl Lambard married Governor Baldwin; Sibyl Lambard's mother was Sibyl Farnham before she married Allan Lambard; Sibyl Farnham's father was William Farnham (b. 1766?), the younger sibling and namesake of the promising boy who died while a student at Harvard; William Farnham's father was Daniel Farnham (1719-1776), for years a lawyer in Newburyport, Massachusetts, though he wasn't born there. Daniel Farnham was my four-times-great-grandfather; his son William, my three-times-great-grandfather. Phebe Cobb's introduction to her aunt's journal tells the story of Daniel and William Farnham, her grandfather and her father, who was Katharine Farnham Hay's brother.

Memory insists it was nighttime and very dark outside when I first read Phebe Cobb's narrative and learned about Daniel Farnham of Newburyport, where he was born, and by whom he was schooled.

Memory may be playing false, but it matches the moment to the story. This is what I read about Daniel Farnham:

> His native place was York, Maine. He was born November 15 in 1719 and died at the age of 56 years. He was prepared for college by Mr. Joseph Moody, a clergyman of that place...

I can still feel a Gothic *frisson*, a touch of ghosts inhabiting the night air. This Mr. Moody was Hawthorne's Mr. Moody, no doubt, and Phebe Cobb reports, as must have been common lore, that he wore the hand-kerchief (white, not black as in Hawthorne) because haunted by the memory of his childhood misfortune:

> Mr. Moody was remarkable for his piety, but more remark-able for never appearing, the last years of his life, without his face being covered by a handkerchief. The cause of this singu-lar circumstance was most melancholy. By one of those–I had almost said, common accidents, he had the dreadful misfor-tune, to shoot a lad, of his acquaintance–from that time the deepest gloom settled on his mind, and he refused to be seen, by his most intimate friends. As there were several men, by the same name, he was distinguished by the populace as "Handkerchief Moody."

So my great-great-great-great grandfather had been a pupil of the man whose story was a model for Hawthorne's Mr. Hooper. What were the odds of that?

If that was not strange enough, what followed touched an even deep-er nerve, as if to tell me why I'd been drawn to "The Minister's Black Veil" in the first place, why I'd assigned it in class, why I'd written about it, why I'd said about it what I did. Phebe Cobb goes on:

> I recollect hearing my father William Farnham say that when he was a very little boy, Mr. Moody passed a night at the house of his parents. When bedtime arrived, being a clergyman, he was requested to pray with the family. The child's curiosity was very naturally excited by the singular appearance of the visitor, and he seized the opportunity, when the good man was fervently engaged in his petitions, to creep slowly, and cau-tiously along, and peep under the mysterious handkerchief.

And then, without missing so much as a heartbeat, Phebe Cobb's narrative resumes its formal, measured course:"Mr. Daniel Farnham was an influential man…"

The questions I'd thought were academic took on bones and flesh and blood. How many generations does it take to atone for the sins of the fathers? And what did young William Farnham see when he peeped (a fine Hawthornean word) behind the veil? Phebe Cobb's failure to linger or even pause over the scene is as tantalizing as Hawthorne's story. No doubt her grandfather Daniel Farnham was an influential man, but surely her father's boyish rashness left some mark behind if he remembered the episode so well and described it so vividly to his daughter as he seems to have done. Was William Farnham punished for his peeping? What did Mr. Moody do when the boy saw his face? And did the Farnhams know something about Joseph Moody that history doesn't, something Phebe Cobb doesn't tell? Maybe not. Maybe the Farnhams and Mr. Moody all acted as though nothing out of the ordinary had happened. Maybe everyone pretended young William hadn't seen the forbidden face, anticipating the family reticence that I felt every day growing up six generations later. But whatever may have happened, what was William Farnham's great-great-great-grandson to think, having now stumbled on the story?

The enlightenment mind, which the academy fell heir to, craves explanations, labors to dissolve mystery. A "rational" explanation would be that when I was young, someone told me or read me the story of Phebe Cobb's father and then, having let it drift into dusty corners of unconsciousness, I recovered it in the shape of an essay, being drawn to "The Minister's Black Veil" by a deep familiarity. But I know, as best one can, that this isn't true. Certainly the Carnochans and the Blisses practiced ancestor worship (as this narrative has in more than one way proven), but their rituals took the form of gathering, preserving, genealogizing, of belonging to the Society of the Cincinnati if you were an eldest son or to the Lords of the Manor; or if you were a woman, to the Colonial Dames of America. We didn't worship ancestors by telling old stories. I tried to imagine such a scene. Around a fire, perhaps. But I can't, which is why I think I know that my encounter with "The Minister's Black Veil" was untouched by any ordinary acquaintance.

Where else to look? Some kind of cellular memory? I mentioned the question to a biologist friend who took it tolerantly though with understandable skepticism. But did I really want an explanation? What kind of explanation could add to my understanding? Why struggle to enlarge the hermeneutic circle? The thing didn't happen in order to be explained any more than Moody's veil or Hooper's (or yours or mine). So be content and don't try to explain it. It was "just a coincidence" and the better for that, the gods' revenge on the academic mind.

Coincidence connects the unconnected, asserting not only connection but the promise of identity. What coincides occupies the same space and time. Hardy and Nabokov (odd bedfellows) and other prophets of coincidence are prophets of unity. What are the chances that the person who wrote that inconspicuous essay in an inconspicuous journal saying don't look under Mr. Hooper's veil, should turn out to be the great-great-great grandson of someone who had seen the forbidden face? Weren't what William Farnham knew and what I said not to try to know coincidental? Hadn't we occupied the same space and time?

If the occult were not hidden, it would be something else altogether. It is the raiment with which we clothe the unknown. Hawthorne had provided the explanation in the first place, and I had understood it: don't look for what you know you can't find. In Peter Høeg's novel about Smilla the Greenlander, the inquiring Smilla says: "Deep inside I know that trying to figure things out leads to blindness, that the desire to understand has a built-in brutality that erases what you seek to comprehend." For all that, it is as hard for her as it is for me not to keep on wanting to figure things out. Those fawning obituaries for Henry Porter Baldwin and George Bliss and his son Walter, were they more than mortuarial puffery? Once years ago when Eve's husband, the bishop, was in Detroit, he asked his taxi driver about a statue of Governor Baldwin that came into view. "Oh, yeah," said the driver, "that old crook!" Victorians were notorious livers of secret lives. Was there a woman who bore my grandfather's child after Mattie died? Weren't there dark doings somewhere in the Wendover world of elegant carriages and the wonderful Rolls-Royce? Where did Fred's money go? Why can't I find out more about Gouv's partner who stole the firm's assets? Who was Frances Adele Quintard? What did Mattie die of? How much did Fred invent of the Empire of the Snakes? Were the stories that the three old men told us on the way to Mawere Shamba made up, any of them, just for us? Why was Mawere Shamba abandoned by its people? And, as I wondered at the start, has this been a tale of paradise lost or just an ordinary slice of the human comedy, told by a more than ordinarily lucky post-Victorian Victorian? Swift, dying, was overheard to say "I am what I am." That answer, godlike or no, is the only one we have. But there's another question: what now? Gibbon ended one draft of his autobiography, the only one of six that he managed to bring up to the time of writing it, with Buffon's calculation that a man of fifty-four, Gibbon's age at the time, had a life expectancy of fifteen years. For a man of sixty-seven, my age as I write, Buffon calculated a life expectancy of nine years, to which two centuries of medicine have added several more. Odds or no odds, Gibbon died at fifty-six. He'd have been better off not to have wanted to decipher the fates.

I try not to backslide into needing to know the unknowable, and especially not needing to know what passed between me and William Farnham, who in his middle age left New England and moved to Indiana, there to make a new life. That we both went west marks our kinship. And sometimes the scene comes back to me when at the age of five or six or seven a boy in eighteenth-century New England, on a cold evening, seized by devilish curiosity during family prayers, crept cautiously along, being careful not to be noticed by others (so intent were they at their devotions), stole up to the mysterious visitor with the veil over his face, and without any thought of coming generations peeped under it to see what could possibly be there.

Colophon

Design
Chuck Byrne
Chuck Byrne / Design

Typeface
Stone Cycles
Stone Typefoundry

Printing
Shoreline Printing

Bindery
Roswell Bookbinding